D1029478

The Complete
SHIH TZU

JULIETTE CUNLIFFE

RINGPRESS

This book is dedicated to the early pioneers who recognised that there were indeed differences between the Shih Tzu and the Lhasa Apso, and to those present day breeders who strive to see that a clear distinction remains.

RINGPRESS

Published by Ringpress Books Ltd,
Spirella House, Bridge Road,
Letchworth, Herts, SG6 4ET

Discounts available for bulk orders
Contact the Special Sales Manager at
the above address. Telephone (0462) 674177

First Published 1992
© 1992 JULIETTE CUNLIFFE

ISBN 0 948955 47 3

Printed and bound in Singapore
by Kyodo Printing Co

CONTENTS

PREFACE

The more one learns about the Shih Tzu, the more fascinating a breed it becomes. It is my earnest hope that readers of this book will derive even a fraction of the pleasure which I have had from researching and writing about this charming, and perfectly delightful, breed. Undoubtedly the Shih Tzu ranks amongst the great characters of the canine race – long may it remain so.

In compiling this book I have greatly appreciated the interest and support I have received from many highly respected breed experts. My thanks are especially due to Mrs Gay Widdrington, Mrs Dorothy Gurney, Sheila and Tom Richardson, Mrs Audrey Dadds, Michael Harper, Mrs Anne Pickburn, and Lesley and Betty Williams. I should also like to thank the Secretaries of the various breed clubs for their kindness in providing valuable information. To all those who have supplied their much treasured photographs, I am extremely grateful and I should like to express my sincere apologies for having been unable to use them all. Carol Ann Johnson is my long suffering partner in dogs and I have not only to thank her for her patience during many hours of noisy word-processing, but also for providing me with many excellent photographs and for allowing me to leave not only my desk, but also the dining room table, in the most appalling mess on so many occasions. I am indebted to Sylvia Evans for the skilful drawings with which she has provided me. Lastly, no book which I write would ever be complete without a brief word of thanks to The Kennel Club's Library staff and to Clifford Hubbard for his constant interest and support.

JULIETTE CUNLIFFE

Ch. Firefox of Santosha (Ch. Santosha Royal Flush – Ch. Yakee Chang Yeh).
British breed record holder with thirty-five CCs.   *Jean Luc.*

Chapter One

EARLY HISTORY IN TIBET AND CHINA

As with so many of the breeds of Asian origin the history of the Shih Tzu is veiled in a certain amount of mystery, but it is clear that the breed has roots in both Tibet and in China. Now classified as a Chinese breed, there are many breeders who consider it rather more Tibetan than Chinese. Certainly there has been much confusion and intermixing of Chinese and Tibetan breeds through the centuries, and so I feel it highly relevant that we begin by looking at the contact between the two countries and the fascinating roles dogs have played in these regions. In doing so, we shall have a sounder foundation upon which to build our knowledge and interest in that most charming character, the Shih Tzu.

Although, historically, there have been times when the Chinese and Tibetans have co-operated with each other with certain cordiality, since the seventh century there has been strife of one kind and another, and safe passage between the two countries has not always been guaranteed. As acts of diplomacy, Chinese brides, frequently of royal rank, were taken by Tibetan nobles. One of the earliest of these was the Tibetan King Srong-brtsan-sgam-po who, in AD 640, was given a Chinese princess as a bride, as was his brother. It follows that gifts were also exchanged between members of these two great cultures. Mythology abounds in both, and it is important to bear in mind that written historical records in Tibet were not kept until around AD 639. It has been said that the Lhasa Apso, clearly a close cousin of the Shih Tzu, and a breed which is always associated with Tibet rather than China, has been in existence since 800 BC, but without tangible written evidence, it is difficult to substantiate such claims.

Buddhism spread from India into Tibet in the seventh century but not until 1253, the time of Kublai Khan, was it adopted in China. The lion, in its various mythological forms, plays an important part in Buddhism, and although the lion was not a species of animal indigenous to China it was imported there as a gift from Emperors from as early as AD 87. The lion has, over the centuries, been depicted by artists in many different ways, possibly because early artists were not familiar with the real animal and built their own vision of the beast, coupled with the lions they knew from Buddhism. There were no lions at all in Tibet, but it is carved lions which support the Dalai Lama's throne at Lhasa. It is said also in Tibet that the five large curls depicted on the lion's head simulate the flags worn in the ancient head-dress of high officials. A theory, which I prefer to believe, is that Buddha remained so long in motionless contemplation that the snails crawled over his head.

Buddha Manjusri, the god of learning, is said to travel around merely as a simple priest with a small Ha-pa dog which can, in an instant, be transformed into a lion, enabling the Buddha to ride on its back. The Manchu Emperors, regarded as the Sun and Sons of heaven, held Buddha's small dog-lion or lion-dog, in the very highest esteem for they, themselves, were described by their flatterers as symbols of Buddha. The Chinese authorities claim that the name 'Manchu' was based on the Tibetan name, 'Manjusri' – the translation of the Chinese 'Wen Chu', meaning Chinese Buddha. It is the snow lion (Gang Sing), considered king of animals, with which the Shih Tzu and, indeed, the Lhasa Apso, are most closely connected, and so powerful is the snow lion that when he roars seven dragons are said to fall out of the sky. He also has the ability to leap and turn instantly, to walk in both mist and cloud, and he has the voice of the Middle Way (of truth and of fearlessness) which subdues all.

The reason that Tibet is considered the earliest ancestral home of the Shih Tzu is because dogs were given as tribute gifts for safe passage from Tibet to China; the journey by caravan took between eight and ten months. In Tibet dogs were never sold but only given as gifts, and it is my personal belief that, in the main, the dogs which made passage to China in this way were largely what we now know in the West as Lhasa Apsos and which were not, as earlier authors have said, sacred animals. They were certainly held in high esteem, but there is no evidence to confirm that the breed has ever had any religious significance, although these little shaggy-coated dogs are said to house the souls of monks who have erred in their previous life of human existence. Buddhists, of course, believe firmly in the theory of reincarnation. Tibetan monks have always distinguished between the "true" lion and the "dog" lion, one being a spiritual beast, his image placed in the sacred places of Buddha, the other, according to Collier, were "earthly ones found in a menagerie." The Tibetans were never too clear about the nomenclature of their breeds, nor did they write books about their dogs. Undoubtedly some crossing took place between the various Tibetan breeds for even now it is possible to mate two pure bred Lhasa Apsos together, or indeed two Shih Tzu, and to produce what to all intents and purposes resembles a pure-bred Tibetan Spaniel!

Small, long-coated Tibetan dogs, of whatever origin, eventually arrived in China and there undoubtedly further crosses took place with breeds of dog which were then already in China. To understand the developments of the Shih Tzu we must therefore look closely at the other small dogs which have been known in that country.

SMALL DOGS IN CHINA

'Square dogs' were accepted by the Emperor Tang as tribute gifts around 1760 BC, but unfortunately we do not know their size and it is likely that these are connected more to the Chow Chow than to the smaller Chinese breeds of today. Around 500 BC (the time of Confucious) it is recorded that when going to the chase, a favourite pastime of the ancient Chinese, one kind of dog followed his master's chariot, while others with short mouths were

A pair of Lion Dogs, one with a puppy, the other with a ball. From the K'Ang Hsi period (1661-1722).

carried in the carts. We can therefore perhaps safely assume that the 'short-mouthed' dogs were quite small. It was said that the nose bones of puppies were broken with a chopstick to make them shorter, but the British Museum houses a skull of a early short-nosed dog in which the naturally short nasal bones are unbroken.

By the end of the first century AD the Emperors had begun to take a serious interest in small dogs and the 'Pai' dog, said to mean a short-legged dog, apparently belonged under the table. This must have indeed been small when one bears in mind that tables were then very low, for people sat on the floor to eat. Great honours were bestowed on small dogs; one belonging to Emperor Ling Ti (AD168) was kept in his garden and, as the Emperor was so fond of his four-legged companion, he awarded the dog the Chow-Hsien grade, the highest literary rank of the period. Many dogs belonging to Emperors were given the rank of K'ai Fu, which is just below that of Viceroy, and the bitches were given the ranks of wives of the corresponding officials. Such dogs were given soldiers to guard them, the choicest carpets to sleep on, and they were fed on only the best rice and meat.

Small dogs were imported into China from Russia and Persia as well as from Turkey. In AD 624 a pair of small dogs were taken from Turkey to China from Fu Lin. Even up to the seventeenth century descendants of these dogs were known as dogs of Fu Lin. Collier in his *Dogs of China and Japan in History and in Art* calculates their measurements as being 7 1/2 inches (19 cm) high by 12 1/2 inches (32 cm) in length. Here we seem to have the Ha-pa dog, which is still known in this century both in China and in Tibet, for one of their colloquial names was 'ha-pa', translated to mean 'pet' or 'lap' dog with short legs. Another name by which it was known was 'Shih Tzu Kou' or 'lion dog'. These little dogs had remarkable intelligence and apparently understood how to carry a torch in their mouths and to drag a horse by its bridle. Collier felt that records showed that in type the dog was probably Maltese in origin, having gone

*Eighteenth Century
Chinese snuff bottle.*

to Turkey from Malta. In the Shantung Province others, referred to as 'ha-pa' and 'Turkish' dogs, were those known as 'pugs' or 'Lo-sze'. Many were short-haired but others were long-coated and were referred to as 'monkey-lion dogs', the local people calling them 'Shih nung kou', meaning fierce, shaggy-haired watch dog. The development of the term 'monkey-lion dog' comes from the legend in which the lion met a small monkey in a forest and fell in love with her. Their disparity in size, however, made their union impossible and so the lion prayed to Buddha to make him small enough to find favour with her, begging also that his great heart would remain intact in order that he might be no less in love. In compassion, the Lord Buddha turned him into a Lion Dog, changing only his stature but not his mighty heart.

In AD 1300 small dogs in China were said to be "golden-coated nimble dogs, which are commonly bred by people in their homes". These were described in historical records as resembling the lion. Incidentally, an Emperor living in AD 1300 loved dogs so much that he regularly used to steal them from his subjects. Berthold Lauffer in his *Chinese Pottery of the Han Dynasty*, published in 1909, tells his readers that 'pug-dogs' were introduced as far as Lhasa where they were called 'Lags K'ye', meaning hand dog. The reason for this was that if a human being were to lay hands on a freshly hatched young eagle, the bird would be transformed into a Chinese pug dog. Between AD 990 and 994 the Lo-chiang dog, another form of 'pug', was sent to the Emperor from the Ssuch'uan Province. These were also described as very small, intelligent, tame and docile. In order that people would be duly respectful to the Emperor, they sat beside him wagging their tails and barking. By 1820 the cult of the lap dog in China reigned supreme, and very tiny dogs, known later as 'sleeve dogs', were the very height of fashion. It is still said that at this time dogs were stunted by artificial means and were reared as dwarf dogs. One of the methods used to restrict growth was limiting the food supply; another was to keep puppies in small wire cages, not releasing them until they had reached maturity. The Dowager Empress Tzu Hsi did, however, object to artificial dwarfing. But fashion, thankfully, is fickle, and soon the sleeve dogs, (kept in the voluminous sleeves) were no longer favoured and were instead referred to as 'lump-headed dogs'.

MARKINGS ON CHINESE DOGS

Great attention has always been paid to colour and markings on Chinese dogs, some being considered fortunate and others quite the reverse. A black or yellow coat and a white head signified the virtual certainty of an official appointment ahead, while the owner of a black dog with white ears was destined to become rich and noble. If he were to have a white dog with a black tail he would ride in a chariot for the rest of his life. The Chinese use the most colourful speech when describing the markings of their dogs, referring to those marked with more than one colour as 'flowered'. One with a 'three-flowered face' has a face which is yellow, black and also white.

THE SLAUGHTER OF CHINESE DOGS

It is generally believed that it was the larger dogs which were used as food in China and, sadly, I know only too well that dog meat is most certainly eaten in China to this day. Thankfully many true Buddhists were vehemently against this custom, and signs appeared outside temples calling on people to avoid the slaughter and eating of dogs, for they were the faithful guardians of their masters' homes. But the pleas of the Buddhists did not stop the killing of dogs and in Manchu there were numerous dog-farms where many of the smaller specimens were raised and sold for their coats.

THE DOWAGER EMPRESS TZU HSI

The Dowager Empress, an infamous, albeit over-indulgent, lover of dogs, was well-known for her involvement with the Pekingese; she was said to have had over a hundred of them. She laid down many rules for the palace dogs, one of which stated that they must be 'dainty in their food' so that by their fastidiousness they might be known as Imperial dogs. The following rules give us an insight into her own fastidiousness!

"Sharks' fins and curlew's livers and breasts of quail, on these may it be fed, and for its drink give it the tea that is brewed from the spring buds of shrub that growth in the province of Hankow, or the milk of antelopes that pasture in the Imperial parks... Thus shall it preserve its integrity and self-respect, for the day of sickness let it be anointed with the clarified fat of a sacred leopard, and give it to drink a throstle's egg-shell full of the juice of the custard apple, in which has been dissolved three pinches of shredded rhinoceros horn, and apply to it piebald leeches."

In her efforts to stub the noses of her Pekingese, the olfactory organs were stroked and massaged, and her dogs were made to chew leather which had been stretched tightly on a frame, this in the hope of acquiring the much desired flatness of face. In 1908 the Dalai Lama, spiritual leader of Tibet, presented several dogs to the Dowager Empress. These were seen by by several foreigners and were described as being similar to the breed of lion dogs seen then in Peking. She considered her 'Shih Tzu Kou' a treasured gift, and she kept them apart from her Pekingese so as to keep them distinct and to maintain their breed characteristics. The Dowager Empress had a preference for 'Imperial Gold' and bred primarily for this colour and for symmetry of markings, especially liking a white mark on the forehead, this being one of the Buddha's superior markings. But the 'Shih Tzu Kou' had arrived only shortly before her death, and although the eunuchs of the palace continued to breed them, it is highly likely that experimental crosses took place causing a divergence of type. It is believed that three short-nosed breeds were bred by the eunuchs in the Imperial palaces, these were the short-haired 'Pug', the Pekingese and the long-haired dog, which we now know as the Shih Tzu. It has also been said that the principal differences between them were in quality and length of coat rather than body shape.

The eunuchs' breeding records were a closely kept secret, and no records or pedigrees appear to have been retained. However, outstanding specimens were depicted on Imperial scrolls, something considered a very great honour, but there were inferior specimens and these found their way into the market place, while others were smuggled out of the palace to be sold either to Chinese noblemen or to foreigners. Slowly the treasured foundation stock of the Empress, given to her by the Dalai Lama of Tibet, was dissipated.

OTHER OPINIONS

In the Tibetan Breed notes of *Dog World*, February 8th, 1952, A. Ferris quotes Brian Vesey Fitzgerald as saying: "I have always understood that it was about 1650 that three temple dogs, holy dogs, were sent to China and that from these three came the Shih Tzus. About a hundred years later, so I have always understood, the then Dalai Lama (and up until this time the temple dog had always been his special property) gave some away to distinguished visitors who were Russians. These dogs were stolen before they had reached the border and about the same time, during a civil upheaval, a good many more disappeared from the Dalai Lama's monastery and reappeared in various parts of the country. From that time onwards all sorts of small dogs bearing some resemblance, however vague, to the Apso of old, became an Apso. It was the end of the temple dog, but it was the start of the monastery dog and also of the caravan dog."

An interesting comment which may have some bearing on the Shih Tzu was made by L. A. Waddell in a record of the 1903-4 expedition to Lhasa: "They are fond of dogs, and especially favour the mongrel breed between the Lhassa Terrier and the Chinese Spaniel." Dr Walter Young in his monograph, *Some Canine Breeds of Asia*, believed there was a great deal of evidence supporting the claim that "the shock-headed variety of small dogs so commonly seen in Peiping are Tibetan in origin."

During the early part of this century there was much conflict of opinion and confusion had arisen. In 1923, when the China Kennel Club was formed in Shanghai, all similar small dogs of this general type were classified as Tibetan Poodles or Lhassa Terriers. Mr A. de C. Sowerby, Editor of the *Chinese Chronicle* and a judge of dogs, wrote in 1930: "It is our opinion that the Tibetan Lion Dog is the result of a cross between the Lhasa Terrier and the Pekingese." He described how all the Tibetan breeds were grouped together, which caused confusion in separating the breeds. At the China Kennel Club Show in Shanghai he had had the Lhassa

Terrier or Tibetan Poodle entered under him, and he had difficulty in deciding which dog to put over another, due to the fact that there was no guidance laid down concerning the breed. He also pointed out that the matter was not aided by the fact that the Tibetan dogs were called by so many different names. In the *China Journal of Shanghai* of February 1933 he made further comment: "It is our opinion that the Tibetan Lion Dog is the result of a cross between the Lhasa Terrier and the Pekingese, which has arisen out of the mixing of the two breeds both in Tibet and China, since the dogs of each country have been taken to the other from time to time by tribute envoys and officials. The cross in Tibet, that has been taken out of that country by way of India, has been called the Apso, while the cross in Peking has been called the Tibetan Poodle, or Lion Dog. Doubtless the Tibetan cross has more of the Lhasa Terrier in it, while the Chinese cross has more of the Pekingese."

The fact that dogs were taken not only from Tibet to China, but also from China to Tibet, is borne out by a comment in Mr Suydam Cuttings' book, *The Fire Ox and Other Years*, for writing of his visit to Tibet in 1937 he also mentions that Chinese dogs were occasionally taken into Tibet where he considered them to be highly appreciated, and there was a "pair of beautiful Chinese dogs" in the 'menagerie' of the Dalai Lama.

In 1934 the Peking Kennel Club was formed, and it scheduled classes for Lhassa Lion Dogs at its shows; the classes were split into those for dogs weighing over 12lbs (5.5kg) and those under that weight. There are some who have staunchly maintained that the Shih Tzu was a breed in its own right in Tibet, and that pure-bred Shih Tzu were presented to Chinese Emperors as long ago as three hundred years. Having personally studied the Tibetan breeds in some depth over a number of years, and search as I might through my very substantial library concerning all aspects of the country, I have found no real evidence which would lead me to go along with those claims. The Tibetans referred to all shaggy-coated dogs as 'apso' or 'apsok', although the word is used primarily with reference to the shorter-legged variety. The Tibetans use the word to denote long hair, and in the Mongolian language it means 'wholly covered – with hair all over'. As the twentieth century progressed we can see that the partial-brachycephalic (partial-short-nosed) dogs which came out of Tibet were different from the brachycephalic ones from China, and in photographic references I have yet to see a small long-coated dog from Tibet resembling the Shih Tzu exported from China.

MADAM LU ZEE YUEN LEE

In 1935 Madam Lu Zee Yuen Lee, a breeder with many years' experience, who drew her knowledge from various sources including old paintings, wrote a most informative and charming account of the *Lhassa Lion Dog* which was published under the auspices of the Peking Kennel Club (KC). The name 'Lhassa Lion Dog' was established by the Peking KC following confusion over the names Tibetan Poodle, Poodle Terrier and Lhassa Terrier, all referring, apparently, to the same breed. Madam Lu Zee Yuen Lee talks of courage and independence which is not pugnaciousness, merely a quality which "makes a dog stick up for his rights to the bitter end. The courage is not combative but it is ever watchful, and woe befall any daring enough to trespass." She considered the independence of spirit to be coupled with 'a quality of affection seldom equalled in any other strain.' These two points in particular, she felt, were what set the breed quite apart from the poodle but likened it more closely with the terrier.

She felt that it "could not easily be pampered, preferring the home it can make itself to that which is made for it." Concern was also expressed that the breed was liable to suffer illnesses if protected from conditions which it could withstand naturally. Described as "just a mass of contrasts as far as the five senses are concerned", Madam Lu thought the breed even-tempered, slow in both sight and in smell, but quick in perception and hearing. She did not witness any exaggerated gestures of affection and thought the Lhassa Lion Dog to be "not intolerant of a caress so much as indifferent." The general behaviour of the breed was aristocratic, and she considered the fact that it was well cared for, even in the poorest quarters, to be indicative of the fine strain from which they had been bred, imposing their qualities upon their surroundings. The Lhassa Lion Dog was, in her opinion, timid but with an affectionate and gentle nature, liking to be with people and to be petted and cuddled. It rarely barked at strangers and when it walked, moved slowly, "like a gold fish swimming in water." The artistic impressions in Madam Lu's little work are perfectly charming and, coupled

Movement like a goldfish.

with her ample descriptions of the various points of the breed, she gives her readers a vivid picture of the way the breed should look through the eyes of the Chinese.

COLOUR AND HAIR

Because yellow was the imperial colour of China, this was "the proper colour of the Lhassa Lion Dog". Those of a uniform colour were called 'Chin Chia Huang Pao', meaning golden armour yellow gown, although the yellow was more like the colour of a camel and if it was of a bright, glossy yellow with stiff strands of hair, then the dog in question was not of pure breed type. Those dogs with a yellow coat and white neck were known as 'Chin Pi Yu Huang', translated as golden cape with a white jade collar, while a yellow coat with a white dome was golden basin upholding the moon, or 'Chin Pan To Yueh' to those more experienced in the native tongue of China. Whipping the embroidered balls ('Pien Ta Shiu Chiu') depicted a dog with round yellow patches and a yellow coat with white tail was 'Yu Chueh Ping', or white jade golden vase. Those with yellow coats and white paws were called 'Hsueh Shan Chin Chin To', or snowy mountain golden camel.

White, actually more of a cream than an ivory white, was rather rare, although if crossed with white European dogs it would be possible to produce more whites though Madam Lu thought their appearance would change, bringing with it either small eyes, pink eyelids, straight noses, pointed mouths, protruding teeth, thin legs, pointed toes or pricked ears. She did say, however, that type could be improved after cross-breeding to the fourth generation. One piece jade ('Yi Kwei Yu') was how a solid white dog was described, but if it had blue eyes it would be glass jade, or 'Po Li Tsue'. A dog which was completely black was called 'Yi Ting Mo', roughly translated as a lump of ink, while black with a white dome was described as jade tip or 'Yu Ting Erh'. The delightfully appropriate description for a dog with a black body and white feet was, standing in snow ('Hsueh Li Chan'). Just as charmingly descriptive was black clouds over snow ('Wu Yun Kai Hsueh') for a dog with a black body coat surmounting not only white feet but also a white belly. One further combination of black with white was the name 'Yu Mo Chuang', or jade davenport, given to a dog with a black back and white legs. The black hair on a Lhassa Lion Dog was inclined to be curly and stiff, sometimes with grey tips.

Dogs which were actually grey, the hair usually being long, thick and curly and with some black and white hair mixed in the coat, were called 'So Yi Wong', with the descriptive translation of the old man in the grass raincoat. The Lhassa dog never had a glossy gold colour, but those called yellow were like the colour of a camel. Dogs which were cream in colour had pink eyes and noses. Yellow or black dogs frequently had some white on their head or body-coat, but not white ears. On the subject of ears Madam Lu remarked that a white dog often had black or yellow ears and a black dog with 'four eyes' had yellow ears. Around the nose the hair was curled and long hair was to cover the corners of the mouth, that under the chin was also long, covering the apron. The coat generally was long, soft and woolly 'like a skein of yarn'. The hair on the legs was to be like a waterfall and not like petals of garlic. Here the hair came down and covered the toes, thus giving rise to the saying 'seeing the legs but not the feet'. Generally the dogs with shorter legs and bodies had very long coats.

Madam Lu found that dogs with stiff hair were comparatively more aggressive and pugnacious

Tassel-like

*Like a
waterfall*

*Petals of
garlic*

than those with a thick woollen undercoat, these being of a milder, gentler nature. Regarding colour, she believed, too, that black or brown dogs with "four eyes" were more ferocious than those which were all white or all yellow. Madam Lu considered dogs more valuable than bitches, and she felt that they should have been bred in Peiping because the Tibetan-bred dogs were heavy and more ferocious, while those from Peiping were light and more gentle. To give Madam Lu's and the various Chinese descriptions of the Lhassa Lion Dog as a relatively coherent whole, I have made a list of the points given by Madam Lu regarding the appearance of the breed and have incorporated the charming and delightfully vivid Chinese drawings:-

Head round and flat.

owl face

lion head

*water chestnut
face*

Mouth flat and short; not pointed.

water caltrop mouth

frog mouth

charcoal heater mouth

Upper lip to cover lower lip. Tongue oval; not pointed.Teeth all inside the lips; not exposed except when expressing joy.

peony petal tongue

Nose flat. A stop at the bridge of the nose. Bunches of hair growing around the nose.

Ju Yi (sceptre) nose

Lin Tse nose

Eyes big, protruding and brilliant. Eyelids smooth and of one colour.

bell eyes

dragon eyes

apricot eyes

Long hair under chin covering apron.

Ears large and pendulous (not standing up).

Kwantung gourd ears

Palm leaf fan ears

Body straight. Abdomen tight. Chest low.

Bear torso

Kneading board body

Tiger back

Legs short and thick.

*Penbrush
holder legs*

*Incense
burner front*

Elephant leg

**Toes round and not pointed (the
shape of mountain ranges). Five
toes to each foot.**

*Plum blossom
paws*

Camel hoof

Tail curled and short.

Feather duster tail

Chrysanthemum tail

Pheonix tail

Coat long, soft and woolly. A layer of thick, woolly undercoat close to the skin.

Colour uniform and 'not mixed'.

**Mixed colours evenly distributed; not one-sided. (Mixed colours evenly
distributed on one side only considered 'one sided beauty'.)**

FAULTS

Small head.
Long pointed mouth.
Narrow nose.
High bridged nose.
No hair around the nose.
Small eyes.
A pointed, narrow tongue.
Protruding lower lip.
Protruding teeth.

Chin without hair.
Small or straight ears.
Curved body and pot belly.
Long legs and high chest.
Pointed toes.
Four toes on hind feet.
Long tail.
Broken or 'flowery' colour.

To emphasise the typical points of the breed, Madam Lu told her readers what should and should not be seen in good specimens. The head was to be seen but not the face, as should the ears, but not the eyes which were covered by hair. The eye-balls, which protruded, were to be seen but not the eye-lids, for if the eye-lids but not the eye-balls were seen, the dog would look like a monkey. The nose was to be seen, but not its bridge due to the deep stop. The upper lip was to cover the lower so that only the upper lip might be seen. With the mouth closed the teeth were not to be visible, but the tongue was to be seen when the mouth was open; the tongue being easily exposed because the nose was 'dented'. Protruding teeth were thought to make a dog look very ugly, but when the dog expressed joy by showing both upper and lower teeth it looked very pretty. Because it was covered by the long hair of the chin, the apron was not seen. In the case of the neck, the nape of the neck was to be seen, but not the actual neck; a long neck not being considered attractive.

Moving on to the body of the dog, Madam Lu wished to see the back, which was to be broad and thick, but not the waist which was short. The tail tip was to be seen but not the tail. It is difficult to comprehend her precise meaning on this point, but she clarified it by saying that "the hair on the tail tip should be long, and the tail itself short". The long hair of the legs, which was like tassels, was to cover the feet so that the legs could be seen but not the feet. This was why the hair was not to grow on the feet "like petals of garlic" for, being coarse, stiff and growing obliquely, the feet would still be seen. While the paw could be seen, the toes could not, for the hair was to cover the toes making them indistinguishable. The spaces between the legs were to be covered with hair so that the body might be seen, but not the belly. The thickness and length of the hair meant that the skin was entirely covered; the hair could be seen but not the skin. Finally, although the woollen undercoat could be seen, it was to cover the flesh so that the flesh could not.

Madam Lu, most interestingly, gave her account of what happened when various colours of the Lhassa Lion Dog were crossed with the Pekingese:

Black Lion Dog/Pekingese – puppies would have big heads and a thick glossy coat. The white hair around the neck, in the tail and on the toes would be longer than the black hair. Additionally, the toes, instead of being round would become pointed.

Yellow Lion Dog/Yellow Pekingese – puppies produced from this mating would have deep yellow, glossy hair, but the coat would be stiff. The hair around the mouth and ears would be dark brown in colour. The name given to dogs from a mating such as this was 'Lychee Hung'.

Lion Dog/ 'medium long-haired' Pekingese – such puppies were rarely grey or white but would usually be "black-yellow" or brown. Alternatively they could be black and yellow in which case they would have "four eyes". The puppies would have long hair around the ears and on tail and legs, but on the body and around the head it would be short, stiff and curly.

Lion Dog/ 'short haired' Pekingese – puppies would have a coarse, hard coat with long hair around the ears and on the tail and legs. In colour, grey or white would be rare, most being black and yellow. The name given to them was 'Chuan Yang Kou', meaning mixed breed.

A further combination given by Madam Lu was Lhassa Lion Dog crossed with a Wonk, this being the name given to a mongrel in China. Once again no grey or white puppies would result from such a mating, but most would be black and yellow with 'four eyes'. They would have 'long mouths', pointed noses, small ears, short legs and long thick hair. These were considered to be the 'lowest type of Lhassa dogs' and were called bench dogs or 'Pan Teng Kou'. Indeed, Madam Lu was at pains to point out the significant differences between the Lhassa Lion Dog and the Pekingese, noting the round toes of the former not pointed like a fox as on the Pekingese. The Lhassa dog waddled as it walked, while the Pekingese either trotted or jumped. She described how, when using the fingers to comb the two breeds' long coats, the Lhassa dog's coat would get 'all snarled up, forming dents and ridges', while the hair of the Pekingese would retain its shape. She likened the muzzles of Lhassa dogs' whelps to those of donkeys, being not round like new-born Pekingese.

Some customary Chinese names for the breed

For dogs with white domes: *Ting Erh*, meaning top child.
Dogs of yellow colour: *Chueh Tse*, meaning tangerine or Hsing Erh, meaning apricot.
Brown dogs: *Li Tse*, meaning chestnut.
Black dogs: *Hsiao Hei*, meaning small black.
White dogs: *Mien Hua*, for cotton, *Hsiao Hsueh Pai Tse*, meaning small, snow-white child or *Yang Tse*, meaning lamb child.
Dogs of more than one colour: *Hua Tse*, translated as flowery child.
Dogs of mixed colours: *Hsiao Ping*, meaning peace or *Hsi Tse*, for happiness.
For a dog taken home from elsewhere: *Lai Tse*, meaning come child.
For male dogs a favourite is *Hsiao Tse*, a boy.
For a bitch: *Niu Tse* or *Hsaio Ya*, a girl.
  Certain words are avoided such as Fu (blessings) and Lu (prosperity) for they could be confused, due to their phonetic sound, with the word Lu, meaning deer – the dog of which we speak should not resemble a deer! The same applies to the word Shou, meaning longevity because the word Shou also means leanness and the Chinese do not require their Shih Tzu to be lean either.

DOGS IN THE MIND OF THE CHINESE

Dogs think and understand; they have the same passions and feelings as men. In this belief the Chinese could conceive that dogs changed into men and men into dogs. In the royal palace in the year 701 there was a body of Imperial guards, called imagi-no-hayato, whose duty it was to bark like dogs on special occasions. They performed their task in order to drive away evil spirits or ghosts. When a foreigner arrived at Court there was no prescribed number of barks but when the

Chinese Emperor drove over the frontier they had to bark twice.

The Chinese consider that a stray dog coming into the home is a symbol of future prosperity and good luck for the family. The dog in China (as well as in Japan) is attributed with magical healing powers. Pieces of paper, stamped with the head of a dog, could be bought for a high price from the temple-keeper. The charm was to be taken home and burnt and was considered efficacious in causing someone to become obedient to the will of another, or, in more extreme cases, to become stupid or to die. The ashes of the burnt charm were either placed in the unwitting recipient's food, put in his tea or were smeared on his clothing. There were, though, occasions when the charm recoiled on the very same individual who was placing the charm, or, most unfortunately, on someone who happened to be near at the time. A yellow charm which had dogs' heads stamped on it was used in a similar way by ladies of easy virtue who desired a rich guest to return to them. The burnt ashes of the charm were mixed in the gentleman's drink or alternatively could be burnt following his departure, provided that the lady uttered the words "upon it as a dog to follow him wherever he may go". In doing so, she was assured that he would indeed return at some time in the future.

A picture of Chang Hsien, a gentleman with a long beard, a bow and arrow and a young boy at his side, was hung in the sleeping apartments of many old Chinese families. With the bow and arrow Chang Hsien was to shoot the 'Heavenly Dog', alias the Dog Star, for if the fate of the family was under this star there would be no son. He was the patron saint of child-bearing women and, under the Sung Dynasty, was worshipped by women who desired children. There have been numerous references to the 'Heavenly Dog'. In AD 561 a 'celestial' dog was said to have come down to earth, and many ceremonies were performed to counteract the ill which had resulted from this visit. Indeed, the 'Heavenly Dog' has long been feared and is said to descend from the heavens to steal the livers of men. A dog with five toes on all four feet is said to be lucky and the dog a good specimen.

DOGS FROM THE BUDDHIST VIEWPOINT

Undoubtedly Tibetan Buddhists treat their dogs with much greater kindness than do the Chinese and Indian peoples. The reason for this is largely because those who follow Buddhism believe in the theory of re-incarnation, and so they may well have been animals in their previous lives or may come back again as animals, for re-birth on the human plane is not frequent. Thus it is that the dogs they see around them may equally have been humans, even relatives or friends of theirs, which have been reincarnated as canines. Every living being is treated with respect and Buddhists refrain from taking life, even a troublesome flea being carefully removed rather then killed. Because a Buddhist will not take life, neither should he put an end to the life of a dog which is suffering. From a personal point of view, this is the one aspect of Buddhism with which I find it difficult to come to terms. The pariah dogs of the streets, which have a miserable existence, are said possibly to be the reincarnations of monks who have been faithless to their vows. The Temple of Reincarnation at Samye had an underground chamber and hanging from the roof of the doorway to the chamber were skins of dogs which had been stuffed with straw. These were dogs which had given good and faithful service to the monks, and their skins were hung like this in the hope that they would be rewarded by reincarnation to a higher plane, assisted by the Distributor-of-Souls.

A devout Buddhist priest once had a dream in which he saw numberless dogs and heard a loud voice saying, "There are no real dogs on earth, but beings temporarily transformed into dogs in order to come into closer connection with you." Dogs are credited with having a soul and there is, on spiritual grounds, no essential difference between dog and man. In early Chinese tombs there are many representations of the dog, both in clay and in pottery, these having been placed there by Buddhists for Buddhism reached China from India and from Tibet.

Dogs taken on sacred pilgrimages and circumnambulations of holy places are thought to be a receptacle for those evil spirits which might have been displeased by the dogs' masters. Many pilgrims used to circuit the five mile ring-road around Lhasa and often, when the masters had died, the dogs continued to make the circuitous route until they, too died. The life of the dog in Tibetan Buddhist cultures is closely interwoven with that of man for his body is used to give warmth and his coat is spun to make into clothing, while the dog's bark warns of intruders approaching. Some dogs in Tibet, albeit not Shih Tzu, are known as Corpse Dogs for they roam wild and exist much like jackals, on what they can find. Because of the means of disposal of human remains in Tibet they have, or at least had until the Chinese invasion, the opportunity to eat those dead which were laid out on mounds outside the villages. If a body is eaten quickly by dogs it is a sign that the soul will move onwards swiftly. In *The Kennel Gazette* of September 1890 Mrs J. Murray Aynsley comments that "The ownerless wandering dogs devour the poorer classes, while the rich are eaten by more distinguished animals."

There is a Tibetan proverb which says: "you must never strike a dog you may have called to yourself", which can be interpreted literally or can be taken as meaning that one should never offend an invited guest, even if he is bad. Certainly to throw a stone at a dog or to strike a dog is considered to be a personal insult by the nomads. A stranger approaching a nomad's tent is to call out so that those inside may know of his approach and call off the dogs, following which he may approach. It is also considered ill-mannered and offensive to suggest that a nomad should sell an adult dog for although he may make a present of a puppy to friends, he will not part with an adult dog. The nomad does not endow the dog with any form of religious adoration.

There are many occasions where early writers have referred to the enormous number of dogs amongst Buddhist communities and I, too, can vouch that this is so in this present day and age, at least in areas where Chinese influence has not taken hold. Huc and Gabet in their *Travels in Tartary, Thibet and China* (1844-1846) said of the dogs in Lhassa, "These animals, in fact, are so numerous in that city that the Chinese contemptuously say that the three great products of the capital of Tibet are Lamas, women and dogs."

Chapter Two

THE BREED LEAVES CHINA

Before discussing the dogs which actually came out of China, I should like to highlight some comments made by the Hon. Mrs McLaren Morrison, writing about Asiatic dogs in *Our Dogs* on July 13th, 1895. She talked of the Japanese Spaniel and of what she called the 'Nepalese Spaniel', saying that the two closely resembled each other in colouring, both being generally black and white, but the Nepalese Spaniel being larger, never smaller than the King Charles. Later she mentions the 'Chinese Spaniels', "much resembling the Japanese and Nepalese, except in colour, as they are of a deep orange, or brindled." Although she had heard that some were small enough to be put in the pocket, she said they were never as tiny as the small Japanese specimens. She thought them very handsome, "their coats being thick and flowing and their faces rather short." Mrs McLaren Morrison thought they were also called 'lion dogs' and certainly felt that they bore a resemblance to the king of animals. It is, of course, possible that she was referring to the Pekingese, but she describes the face as "rather short" which makes me wonder whether the dogs she saw might possibly have been early representatives of the Shih Tzu.

Lady Brownrigg had married her husband (who later became General Sir Douglas Brownrigg) in 1919, and it was at the time of his posting to the North China Command as Assistant Adjutant and Quartermaster General that they managed to acquire their first Shih Tzu. This was in 1928. They had heard that what they described as 'Tibetan Lion Dogs' or 'Shock-dogs' were owned by the Emperors, having been given as tribute gifts by Tibet's Dalai Lama. The Brownriggs lived in Peking and understood that the best ones were to be found there, and having seen a small black and white one which took their fancy they determined to get one similar. Sadly the first bitch they acquired died in whelp, but soon, with the help of Madam Wellington Koo, they found another black and white bitch, born in 1927. Small, with a white 'apple mark' on her head and a black patch on her root of tail and her side, she was named 'Shu-ssa'. With her large, expressive

A Chinese Ha-pa dog kept by Tibetan Lamas at one of their monasteries in Pokhara, Nepal, 1991.
J. P. A. Cunliffe.

eyes and her hair sticking out around her face she was said to have looked like a fluffy baby owl or a chrysanthemum. Her coat was thick and her tail curled quite tightly over her back. But Tibetan Lion Dogs were not generally seen in public places, for they were kept primarily in the homes of the Chinese and in their courtyards. The Palace eunuchs were also said to have some, and others had been bred by a few French and Russian people living in China. In the Brownriggs' search for a mate for Shu-ssa they came across some large, coarse dogs with either black or dark grey coats, a few others were gold in colour but their aim was to find another particolour. Dr Cenier, a Frenchman, owned a small, rather lightly-built black and white dog, who was a proven sire. He had a good tail carriage, good movement and a straight, soft coat and was described as "very active, a great character and sportsman." When Dr Cenier returned home, this young dog came into the possession of the Brownriggs and was named Hibou.

Around the same time Miss E. M. Hutchins had acquired a dog named Lung-fu-ssu, whelped in 1926. He was a heavier white and black dog with a coarser, somewhat wavy coat, and his tail was carried rather loosely. Miss Hutchins returned to England in 1930, bringing the Brownriggs'

The Abbot of Shekar Cho-Te with a Lama holding a Chinese Ha-pa dog (right). Photo from 'The Epic of Mount Everest' by Sir Francis Younghusband, published 1926.

Photo courtesy Carol Ann Johnson.

two dogs, Lung-fu-ssu and a bitch called Mei Mei who, after she came out of quarantine, was sadly killed by a Sealyham. The weights of the three surviving specimens, known as Tibetan Lion Dogs, were: Shu-ssa 12lbs 1oz, Hibou 13lbs 10oz and Lung-fu-ssu 14lbs 9oz. Lady Brownrigg was aware that there were other, smaller dogs in China, but she said that they were not used for breeding. Shu-ssa had been mated to Hibou as planned and produced her first litter in quarantine, in April 1930. At that time the puppies could be collected from the quarantine kennels at the age of eight weeks. One of these puppies, Tai-tai, went to Miss Hutchins and became the dam of several litters. Two dogs from that first litter, Ting and Popen, went to Lady Brownrigg's parents, General and Mrs Jeffries, and a bitch, Sungari, went to one of her childhood friends, the Hon. Mrs Robert Bruce, living in Scotland. Lady Brownrigg returned to England in 1931, and in the same year Shu-ssa produced a second litter, this time to Lung-fu-ssu. Her third and last litter, a repeat mating to Hibou, was born in 1932.

During this time Col. and Mrs Bailey were much involved in acquiring Apsos. Col. Bailey had taken over from Sir Charles Bell as political officer for Tibet in 1921. In 1928 the Baileys brought back six Apsos to England, five of which were direct descendants of their original pair, which had been presented to Mrs Bailey while she was living in Sikkim on the Tibetan frontier

*Miss Hutchins'
Lung-Fu-ssu
(left) and Tang
(right), pictured
in the early
1930s.*

Guiver.

in 1922. Mrs Bailey observed that the "Lhassa Terriers' in the interior of Tibet and near the Indian border had narrower skulls and longer muzzles and were generally more terrier-like than the Apsos found in the monasteries near the Chinese border, where they generally had shorter legs and shorter muzzles and were rather more round in eye." Could these just possibly have been Shih Tzu?

By now there were a number of small long-coated dogs in the UK and so the 'Apso and Lion Dog Club' was formed and was recognised by the Kennel Club. The first show to hold a class for the 'breed' was the West of England Ladies Kennel Club Show in 1933, and it was immediately apparent that the dogs were very different, especially in the varying length of foreface. Col. Bailey, who was judging, made no secret of the fact that he thought the dogs from Peking were of a different breed; he expressed his belief that they had been crossed with the Pekingese. The 'battle of the noses' had begun! The battle raged for several months, and there is still contention around the world today, though a blind eye is regrettably turned by some. I am fortunate enough to have access to an enormous amount of correspondence which was exchanged between the various parties concerned, and I believe that in the interests of both breeds it would be helpful to quote from some of the letters in order to take a closer look at the beginnings of the two breeds outside China.

On February 12th, 1934, General Brownrigg wrote to Lieut. Col. F. M. Bailey: "Although we have never met I am writing to you in the hope that this letter may assist towards settling the present difficulties over Apsos." He went on to describe how his wife had joined him in China in 1927 and how a certain Colonel Haskard "had a Tibetan Lion Dog which he had bought some time previously in Peking. This was the first dog of its kind that my wife or I had ever seen. We shortly afterwards went from Shanghai to Peking and there saw several of these dogs. We bought

The Cheltenham Show, 1933, before the breeds were sorted out. Left to right: Lady Brownrigg with Hibou, Yangste and Shu-Ssa, Miss Hutchins with Lung-Fu-ssu and Tang, General Sir Douglas Brownrigg with Hzu-Hsi and Miss Marjorie Wild with one of her Apsos.   Guiver.

one of these in 1928 (a bitch). In 1929 we again went to Peking and were on the look-out for a dog to mate with our bitch, and came upon a dog known as Brownie, which we very much liked, but which was not for sale. The Teichmans told us that Mrs Bailey, during a visit to Peking, had also very much liked this dog. This was the first time we had heard Mrs Bailey's name mentioned, but we subsequently learned that she had imported several dogs into England, and rather naturally we assumed they were like ours, basing this supposition on the appearance of the dog, Brownie. As we could not acquire Brownie, we bought another dog as a mate for our bitch from a relative of the manager of Wagons-Lits-Hotel in Peking. This is the history of our original pair. Colonel Haskard subsequently also bought a bitch in Peking, which fitted him out with his original pair.

"Our dogs preceded us to England by a year, and the first litter was born in quarantine at the Blue Cross Kennels in 1930. When we came back to England in 1931 we were naturally very anxious to meet Mrs Bailey and get our dogs registered – Mrs Bailey having in the meantime registered hers as Apsos. My wife and I went twice to see Mrs Bailey in 1931 in London, once before and once after seeing her dogs at Sheerness. We were rather surprised to find amongst the dogs at Sheerness only two (puppies) which had short noses like ours. On the second visit to Mrs Bailey we brought photographs of our dogs and asked her about the obvious difference in the length of the nose. At this interview Mrs Bailey said more than once "the shorter the nose, the better." Mrs Bailey was then kind enough to write across the back of one of our photographs that she considered the dogs to be Apsos. Armed with this photograph, with Mrs Bailey's writing on the back, we went to the Kennel Club, and got our dogs registered as Apsos. I may say that we never much cared for the word Apso, but naturally accepted it, as Mrs Bailey had been the first in the field. Since then the Apsos have gone ahead. I personally have a list of over twenty owners in England with dogs of our type (by no means all of whom have bought their dogs from us or from Colonel Haskard). We first showed a pair of our dogs at Hereford in 1932, and it was solely due to the stir they caused there that we managed to get a class for Apsos (the first class for this breed in England) at a show in Cheltenham in the beginning of 1933. At this show one dog appeared with a longer nose, belonging to Miss Wilde [Wild], which she had bought from Dudley.

"So much for the past. I fully realise that it must be very annoying to you to find our short-nosed variety in the field registered under the name of Apsos, but I do at the same time suggest that in view of the past history which I have outlined above, it is too late for us to go back. Even were it possible to get owners of our type to cancel their registration as Apsos it would do your type no good, as it would so largely reduce the actual numbers registered, and from our point of view we would feel we had unwittingly let down people to whom we had sold our type. For the future, therefore, may I suggest that we get the Kennel Club to recognise both types under the heading of Apsos and that we differentiate them by the names 'Apsos, Chinese Type,' and 'Apsos, Tibetan Type'?"

General Brownrigg finally suggested that the Baileys and the Brownriggs meet to form a committee for "standardizing the points of both types." However, by April 3rd of that same year General Brownrigg had written to the Kennel Club to confirm that they accepted the KC's advice and agreed to separate their dogs entirely from Apsos and to re-register them as Shih Tzu. In the same letter he did, though, take the opportunity of pointing out that Col. Bailey would be judging at the Ladies Kennel Association show that year, and that as he and his wife were the importers of the 'long-nosed type' it would obviously be useless for the Brownriggs to produce their "type in the hope of being successful ....".

In subsequent correspondence Col. Bailey said he realised that it was impossible to judge Shih Tzu and Apsos in the same class, but thus it would have to be until a separation were to be accomplished. Under the circumstances it was against his wish to judge at the LKA that year, but he could see no way out of it and felt that the same difficulty would confront any judge. Certainly in those very early days, judging both breeds as one posed something of a challenge, and the judge's critique of 'Apsos' at Crufts in 1934 read: "One white dog which took my fancy in the ring very much at first glance, I could not place on examination. The round eye, domed head and flat face, also the tail made it of different type altogether, the outlook being nearer to that of the Japanese Spaniel or Pekingese. Though I did not know this at the time, I ascertained afterwards this dog had been bred from a dog and bitch imported from China."

To add to the problem there was contention as to whether or not the Shih Tzu, as it was to be called, would still be considered a Tibetan breed. On April 24th, 1934, General Brownrigg wrote to Col. Bailey: "When our type is re-registered as Shih Tzu the breed will still be Tibetan – just as much as an Irish Terrier is a British breed, although Southern Ireland is now a free State. Tibet was part of the Chinese Empire until very recent years." The debate continued and Mona Brownrigg entered into correspondence with Lady Freda Valentine who, with her husband, tried to smooth things over. Despite the agreed change in name, there was difficulty in getting Shih Tzu owners to drop the word 'Tibetan'. Many owners continued to refer to their breed as 'Tibetan Lion Dog', prompting the Tibetan Breeds Association to write to the Kennel Club protesting that 'the use of this epithet Tibetan should not be permitted to a type of dog which, although perhaps originally Tibetan, and which may still be called by Europeans on the coast of China, has been so long bred in China that it has lost its original true Tibetan character.' The Association had not, however, objected to the following announcement in *Kennel Gazette* of July 1934, for the Baileys had been in Finland at the time.

"The following application will be considered by the Committee of the Kennel Club at their meeting in September. Any person, Club, Association or Society having objection thereto should communicate with the Secretary as soon as possible."

Shih Tzu (Tibetan Lion Dog) Club, Mrs M. Brownrigg.

In September of that year the *Kennel Gazette* carried the announcement: "The application to change the title of the Apso and Lion Dog Club to Shih Tzu (Tibetan Lion Dog), was granted."

The Kennel Club refused to listen to the plea of the Tibetan Breeds Association until General Brownrigg returned from America. Francis Valentine wrote to Col. Colenso at the Kennel Club in January of 1935 explaining what had happened to date and commenting that: .... "the Lhasa Apsos and the Shih Tzu had both been known as Apsos or Tibetan Lion Dogs and the difficulty in judging the two together was one of the main factors which led to the formation of the Tibetan Breeds Association. After the split the two breeds were re-registered with the KC as 'Lhasa Apsos' and 'Shih Tzus' respectively. Also the Tibetan Breeds Association has always maintained that the Lhasa Apso is the true Tibetan Lion Dog but it was felt that the latter name is such an attractive one that it must be discarded by all parties as an official nomenclature in the interests of harmony."

On October 12th, 1934 the Hon. Mrs Irma Bailey had written to the KC saying: "All we ask is that the owners of the Shih-tzu (a dog imported from China) should not be permitted by the Kennel Club to use with reference to their club this word 'Tibetan' which they are not permitted to use with reference to their breed of dog. The Tibetan Breeds Assocn. was formed with the object of clearing up the confusion among breeds of Tibetan dogs in this country; the Shih-tzu being a dog imported from China was, for that very reason, deliberately excluded; and owners of this breed withdrew from the Tibetan Breeds Assocn. The object of the Tibetan Breeds Assocn. i.e. the control and encouragement of Tibetan breeds will be frustrated by the use of the word "Tibetan' with reference to a dog of very distant Tibetan origin. No dog of the Shih-tzu type has as far as we know, ever been seen in Tibet; the Shih-tzu is now predominantly Chinese although it may possibly have had a remote Tibetan ancestry; ... Moreover it has been imported from China and not from Tibet."

The pages of correspondence continue in much the same vein, and on February 20th, 1935 the Secretary of the Kennel Club wrote: "I beg to confirm the decision of the Committee of the Kennel Club that the registration of the title Shih Tzu (Tibetan Lion Dog) Club has been cancelled." At this time Miss Hutchins and the Brownriggs co-operated closely concerning the breeding of Shih Tzu in the UK, detailing all important facts about every puppy born and inspecting litters whenever possible. Puppies which were not of a sufficiently high standard were sold as pets. The Shih Tzu Club grew in strength, with General Brownrigg as Treasurer of the Club and Lady Brownrigg as Secretary.

SNIPPETS FROM THE PRESS OF THE 1930s

FOREIGN DOG FANCIES – *OUR DOGS* – January 23rd, 1931

"... last year there was an application made to the KC General Committee for the registration of what the owner called Tibetan Lion Dogs. I had never previously heard of Tibetan Lion Dogs and apparently the KC General Committee were equally in the dark about them, as the Committee met the request by 'suggesting' that the owner register the Lion Dogs as Tibetan Spaniels. Now here again we have a very old-established breed and one long familiar to the British fancier, so whatever the Lion Dogs were, there should have been no difficulty in knowing at a first glance whether or not they were Tibetan Spaniels. But apparently there is no first glance where Foreign Dogs are concerned; there is apparently and practically a blind registering of such breeds."

Geo. Horowitz

FOREIGN DOG FANCIES – *OUR DOGS* – MAY 1st, 1934

"It was at Cheltenham show, that charming classic of the W.E.L.K.S., that Shih Tzus had the biggest entry they have yet put up in this country... Mrs Gardiner and her executive have provided four classes for the breed, which will be judged by Mr A. G. Nichols. The guarantors are the Shih Tzu Club, Mrs Brownrigg, Mrs Eaden and Miss Reoch."

Will Hally

FOREIGN DOG FANCIES – *OUR DOGS* – June 22nd, 1934

"I have previously remarked that the little mix-up between the Apsos and Shih Tzu is damaging the prospects of both these breeds at the moment. But at the weekend I heard from several owners of Tibetan Terriers and Tibetan Spaniels that their breeds are also being affected by the controversy, though they do not come into it. Apparently judges are chary of having anything to do with Tibetan canines while the Apso-Shih Tzu affair is on, and this is making exhibiting very discouraging. .... I want it to be clearly understood at the outset, however, that while the Apso and Shih Tzu devotees are both standing by their guns, there is no ill-feeling on either side. It is, right through, a thoroughly sporting controversy... However, it was eventually decided to appeal to the Kennel Club to grant the name of Shih Tzu to the Chinese dogs, and to my mind that is infinitely preferable. To differentiate the two by mere 'type' would have led to a permanent hotch-potch, with the added difficulty of judicial preferences coming in – for the short-nosed or other 'type' as the case might be... I must emphasise that it was solely on the initiative of General and Mrs Brownrigg that the Shih Tzu were taken out of the Apso category and placed where they now are, and that was done solely to avoid any clash with the Apso people. It does therefore seem very unkind that the Shih Tzu people having gone that length, should be asked to go still further. But, and although I do not like the job, I am bound to point out that the Apsos had prior claim to the title of Tibetan Lion Dogs; that in itself does not matter very much because the Apsos are not claiming that as their alternative title. The other fact which decides me to write as I am doing is that Tibetan Lion Dog is purely a Chinese name – it is not a Tibetan one, in the sense that it is not used in Tibet. There is also this fact that a British ruling, whatever the ruling may be, does not affect owners on the China coast, in France or in Scandinavia. It affects only the British dog fancy. As I see the situation, too, the Shih Tzu, whatever its origin, is now more a Chinese than a Tibetan breed – in its Chinese form it is not met with in Tibet."

Will Hally

FOREIGN DOG FANCIES – *OUR DOGS* – 19th October, 1934
Re: Impressions of the KC Show

"The Shih Tzu was Madame Arline's familiar winner, Tai-ping Llama... I don't know that I really expected a better turn-out of Shih Tzu, as the specialist club for this breed has only recently been registered; it has not got into working order yet, and besides that, and although there are plenty of Shih Tzu about, there is the general feeling that a breed such as this stands only a meagre chance in mixed company, and looks to the future and to separate breed classes."

Will Hally

FOREIGN DOG FANCIES – *OUR DOGS* – December 13th, 1935

"The Shih Tzus and their own specialist club are also definitely on progressive lines, and with 14 registrations, these alluring Chinese products have any amount of material, and very decidedly they are catching on. I place them alongside the Tibetans as future certainties, and the Shih Tzus look like giving some of the Tibetans a good race for the popularity stakes."

Geo. Horowitz.

THE SECOND WORLD WAR

The war years interrupted not only breeding and showing activities but also the importation of new stock. However, by the close of 1939 a total of one hundred and eighty-three Shih Tzu had been registered with the Kennel Club. 1940 was an important year for the breed, for instead of being registered under 'Any Other Variety' it was granted a separate register, becoming eligible for Challenge Certificates, though none were awarded until after the war.

During the war Lady Brownrigg was much involved with Red Cross work, and wool from the groomings of dogs' coats was made into yarn and used to knit articles which could be sold in aid of the Red Cross. Breeding practically ceased and it was a struggle to preserve the breed which, like others, was in danger of dying out. As soon as the war ended, a few of the original breeders bred from the remaining stock and new imports, and they resumed their showing activities. However, in order to preserve the breed all available dogs and bitches were used for breeding purposes, often regardless of their quality. This is one of the reasons why some of the dogs of that post-war period differ quite substantially from those we see in our show rings today. There was an increase in size and weight in some of the stock, with many becoming too large. In 1945 there were only two Shih Tzu registered with the Kennel Club; one was Ta Chi of Taishan, who was to become the breed's first Champion, gaining her title in 1949. Sired by Sui-Yan and out of Madam Ko of Taishan, she descended from the Norwegian import, Choo-Choo, from Tashi of Chouette and from the first British imports. She is still much renowned, and a great many breed experts feel that she was one of the most typical specimens of the breed and that we should constantly keep her memory fresh in our minds.

Ch. Ta Chi of Taishan (Sui-Yan – Madam Ko of Taishan). Bred and owned by Lady Brownrigg, Ta Chi was the breed's first Champion. She was typical of the sturdy British type.

Photo by Fall, courtesy G. Widdrington.

A Royal Family scene; Choo-Choo is in the foreground.

Studio Lisa.

Ch. Wang-Poo of Taishan (Ch. Choo-Ling – Ch. Pa-Ko of Taishan). Bred and owned by Lady Brownrigg, Wang-Poo and his parents made an important contribution to the breed.
Photo by Fall, courtesy G. Widdrington.

Mr and Mrs Bode returned to the UK in 1945, having first come into contact with the breed when living in what was then Persia. They had an unfortunate introduction to the breed for their first Shih Tzu was stolen and when recovered had to be put to sleep due to injuries from stoning. At this time, Mrs Bode was unfamiliar with the origin of the Shih Tzu; she was enlightened by Monsieur Graeffe, the Belgian Ambassador, who had brought six specimens of the breed with him from Peking, descendants of Lize and Kwanine, a pair bred in the Imperial Palace in the 1920s. One of his dogs was mated to one of Mrs Bode's Pekingese, as there was no available Shih Tzu bitch, and they produced four puppies: Tao-Tzu, Chiang-Tzu, Wang Tai and Kai Tzu. Again the dogs met with misfortune, Wang Tai died of pneumonia as a young puppy, Tao-Tzu was killed in a car accident in Tehran, and Kai-Tzu died while having an operation in Paris. Chiang-Tzu lived to the age of fourteen in Brussels. None of the dogs came back to England with Mr and Mrs Bode, so that when Mr Bode met Sir Douglas and Lady Brownrigg in 1945 he was without any Shih Tzu. It was not until 1948 that Mrs Bode managed to acquire a dog and a bitch, Sing Tzu of Shebo and Shebo Tsemo of Lhakang and later they were joined by Schunde who was a black son of Ishuh Tzu, imported from China by Major General Telfer-Smollett.

Dog World of May 27th, 1949, included an article about the breed written by Sheila Bode and in which she stated: "... They are described in early Chinese writings as 'so completely covered with long hair reaching to the ground that it was impossible to distinguish one end of it from the other.' Very recent information from an authentic source reveals that the Shih Tzu are known as 'The Death-Dragon Dogs' and the cult of these sacred dogs is zealously guarded to this day. They are bred in the monasteries, held absolutely sacred and kept in strict seclusion... The lion-faced 'Dragon Dogs' are bred and trained for specific duties connected with funeral rites, and as these differed so widely from Chinese religious rites it was felt the Emperors, and the Dowager Empress Tzu Hsi in particular, would have been shocked at the gift of a 'Death-Dragon Dog,' so, because of their leonine features the Chinese envoys re-named them the sacred 'Lion Dogs'...."

OTHER IMPORTS TO THE UK

Several Shih Tzu were imported to the UK before the First World War, but many of them were not bred from. In 1933 Choo-Choo was imported from Norway to Queen Elizabeth, and in her

Shih Tzu Handbook Mrs Widdrington remarks that this was "a good black and white, but was overshot with rather a long nose." Fu Tzu and Niu San, bred in 1937 by the Countess d'Anjou, were brought from China by Mrs Audrey Fowler, but there were no progeny. In 1939 a black and white dog of unknown parentage, Ming, was imported from China by Mrs Telfer-Smollett. Tashi of Chouette was one of three dogs imported by Lady Brownrigg and Miss Reoch, from Mr and Mrs Morgan in Canada. The two other dogs died, but Tashi went to the Earl of Essex and she appears to have introduced liver pigmentation.

Following the war, in 1948, Ishuh Tzu (Dandy of Shanghai – Ch-Chu of Shanghai) a gold-brindle and white, was imported from Doreen Lennox in China by Major General Telfer-Smollett. This line seems to have been the first to introduce solid colours. A dog called Wuffles and a bitch called Mai-Ting were also imported from China, but their ancestry was unknown. Mai-Ting, owned by Mr and Mrs Morris, stationed in Shanghai, was given to the Morris's children by the chauffeur of the Ministry car, and she arrived in their household at the age of about six weeks, a minute black and white ball of fluff. She had apparently come from "a Number 1 Chinese family in Yu-Yuen Road." Mai-Ting came back to the UK by cargo ship, and was joined the following year by the Morris family. Wuffles belonged to their friends, the Buchanans. This dog was bred by a German in Peking and was 'camel coloured'. When these dogs were back in England they were mated together and produced a black and white bitch. Sadly, Wuffles was killed by a lorry early in 1952.

EARLY DAYS IN AMERICA

On January 6th, 1936 the KC wrote to Mrs Knapp, Secretary of the Tibetan Breeds Association in the UK, advising her that a letter had been received from the American Kennel Club asking for information regarding 'Lhasa Terriers' and Shih Tzu. The American Kennel Club (AKC) had received an application to register a Shih Tzu and had made a statement that "the Lhassa Terrier and the Shih Tzu are one of the same breed". In response Mrs Knapp sent another copy of the standard of points for the four Tibetan breeds (in case those sent earlier had been "sent away") and closed by saying: "There is a decided difference between the two species. Most noticeable are the large prominent eyes, short almost turned up nose, wide muzzle and Pekingese expression of the Shih Tzu, compared with the smaller eyes, slightly longer straighter nose, and narrower terrier-like muzzle of the Lhasa Apso."

Mr and Mrs Patrick Morgan, who lived in Canada, obtained their Shih Tzu from Peking and Mrs Morgan, in particular, wrote several articles on Apsos and Shih Tzu for the American press, doing much to make both breeds better known in the United States. In an article entitled 'What is a Lhasa Lion Dog?', published in *Town and Country*, probably in 1935 or early 1936, Patrick Morgan writes: ".... It is clear that both the Lhasa Apso (now combined with the Lhasa Terrier) and the Shih-tzu have taken parts and translations of the Lhasa Lion Dog's name; while it took some thirty years to separate the Tibetan Terrier from the Lhasa Lion Dog, the new Lhasa Apso and Shih-tzu separated without hesitation, without prediction.

"This separation, not clearly understood elsewhere, has done much to slow up recognition in other countries; in fact no other country recognises both (the USA and Canada recognize the Lhasa Terrier; Norway recognizes the Shih-tzu). England should clearly state what she has done, that others may know."

Lady Freda Valentine, visiting the USA late in 1936, provided Will Hally with her comments about the Apso and Shih Tzu in America, Mr Hally commenting that "it is such a surprise to find that there is such a fine stock of both breeds there now." In effect, what had happened was that dogs registered as Shih Tzu in the UK had been exported to the USA, where they were incorrectly registered as Lhasa Apsos. This continued until the 1950s. For several years I have been tracing back records though the English Kennel Club, noting dogs which have been registered as one breed and then, later, re-registered as another, due to the early confusion between the various Tibetan breeds and the Shih Tzu. My research in this regard is still on-going, but already I have discovered more dogs re-registered than would appear to have been acknowledged in the USA. In fact, this has had a greater effect on the Lhasa Apso than on the Shih Tzu. However, the early problems did have a negative effect on the Shih Tzu, for they undoubtedly delayed its recognition as a separate breed.

Chapter Three

THE BREED MOVES ON

When the Second World War was over, Lady Brownrigg and Mrs Widdrington (then Mrs Garforth-Bless) working as Secretary and Treasurer respectively, managed to get the Shih Tzu Club active again. As will be appreciated, very few puppies were registered with the Kennel Club during the war. The breed, though, had already produced its first Champion, Ta Chi of Taishan, and during the 1950s several new breeders came into the breed, and were to have a great influence in the years to come. There was an interesting advertisement in *Our Dogs* in October 1950: Alfred Koehn of the Ra Shi kennel planned to leave China and planned to take some dogs with him. This would have been a splendid opportunity for some fresh blood, but hopes were dashed when his plans came to nothing and the dogs had to remain in China.

In the same year Mr and Mrs Kenneth Rawlings arrived in the Shih Tzu show rings with Perky Ching of the Mynd, and the Rawlings' Antartica kennel was to influence the breed in both coat quality and presentation. Mrs Widdrington's Lhakang kennel produced its first Champion, Sheba Tsemo of Lhakang, in 1951, and at the same time Miss Freda Evans of the Elfan kennel acquired a Shih Tzu, Elfann Fenling of Yram, from Mrs Haycock. Lady Brownrigg's Taishans, along with the Lhakang and Antartica bred dogs were highly successful in the coming decade.

THE PEKINGESE CROSS OF 1952

Miss Freda Evans was a breeder of high repute within the Pekingese world before she acquired her first Shih Tzu. Although she was a newcomer to the breed, she felt that certain faults were creeping in, and she believed that she could improve this situation. In her opinion, the breed was too in-bred and she recognised problems of over-size, narrow heads, snipey muzzles, and noses which were too long. She also saw evidence of terrier legs, narrow fronts, loose jointedness, poor coats, near-set eyes and 'bad carriage'. I stress that these were her own opinions, and were not necessarily held by other, more experienced Shih Tzu breeders of that time. Indeed, such 'faults' were disputed by many. Miss Evans' plan was to introduce a Pekingese cross to the Shih Tzu breed, and there were, understandably, some very mixed feelings about this important move. Mrs Widdrington wrote saying that she considered a cross would bring in fewer faults than an imported Shih Tzu of unknown pedigree. Be that as it may, the crossing was carried out without consultation with the Shih Tzu Club, the aim of which was to protect and improve standards. Miss Evans' actions were disputed by many, especially in view of the fact that she did not write explaining the motives involved until after the birth of the puppies.

The dogs she used were her black Shih Tzu, Elfann Fenling of Yram (Ch. Choo Ling – Ch. Sebo Tsemo of Lhakang) and the black and white Pekingese, Philadelphus Suti T'Sun Of Elfann, who was a "good little dog with a perfect mouth". However, he had rather straight legs and that, apparently, was one of the reasons for using him as a stud. The controversy continued for many years and in the *Manchu News Letter* of Spring, 1975 Miss Evans wrote the following in defence of the mating she had carried out some twenty-three years earlier:

"My action at the time of the Peke cross was made known to the Kennel Club and each generation was registered in the *Kennel Gazette* ... Breeders were soon aware of the improvement of the breed, and I feel it is very unkind to stir up this trouble again after twenty-three years, when the breed has reached its present attractiveness and beauty... Some English stock in the early days was becoming unbalanced from inbreeding. The breed was numerically small and the few imports from China were rather big and rangy, also leggy. Many had poor pigmentation and coats, on the whole were poor, although there were some exceptions. Many of the early Shih Tzu lacked charm, balance and quality. As it is now twenty-three years since the cross happened, there are few breeders as old as myself, who really know what the 'oldies' looked like. After all, there are few breeds whose ancestors were pure..."

The cross was quite correctly registered with the Kennel Club and extreme care was taken in the integration of the offspring into Shih Tzu breeding programmes. Only one bitch puppy of each succeeding generation was mated back to a Shih Tzu until the third generation when six puppies were registered and four of these bred from. At this stage they were still cross-breeds, but their progeny were eligible for first class registration as pure Shih Tzu. The six Shih Tzu from that third generation were Ti-ni-Tim of Michelcombe (dog) and Michelcombe Pee-Kin-Pus, (bitch) who went to Mrs Widdrington in the north of England, Elfann Shih Wei Tzu, (bitch) who was transferred to Mrs Murray Kerr in Scotland, Mu Ho, (dog) who went to Mrs Thelma Morgan in the Midlands, and two bitches – Michelcome Fucia and Mitchelcombe Dinkums – remained with Miss O. I. Nichols in Devon; she owned the dam, Yu Honey, who was a cross-breed. The only two of the six not used in future breeding programmes were Pee-Kin-Pus and Fucia.

Extensive breeding was then carried out using this stock, and as one can see from the location of those who owned them, they were well distributed up and down the country. In time, the majority of kennels in the UK had some of this blood somewhere in their pedigrees for it was difficult to avoid in-breeding without actually incorporating it. There were also exports carrying this line, especially to Sweden where Fu-Ling of Clytsvale, exported to Mrs Jungefeldt in 1958, became a strong stud influence. Int. Ch. Golden Peregrine of Elfann was exported to Mrs Belli in Italy, having already gained his title in England. He went on to become one of the most successful English-bred dogs on the continent. In time, the breed certainly did become much more uniform in size; the particularly large specimens were rarely found in the show ring and the

Ch. Jen-Kai-Ko of Lhakang (Sing-Hi of Lhakang – Jessame of Lhakang). Jen-Kai-Ko brings in the Swedish line from Jungefaltets Jung-Ming, and also the last line to come from China via Gun-Yiang of Lunghwa.   Pearce.

very small ones were rarely below 12lbs. However, the Shih Tzu does still have an enormous weight range, given in the current Breed Standard as 10-18lbs. The smaller dogs were generally of sounder construction than they had previously been. It would appear that both the Peke influence and the Swedish lines were instrumental in reducing the overall size. Chinese visitors to England, well aware that large specimens had not been kept in the Imperial Palace, had criticised the size of the British dogs; the biggest had weighed 20-22lbs. Leo Wilson, an all-round judge and editor of *Dog World*, felt that the Shih Tzu should be small, yet solid and low to the ground with a short face. He stated quite publicly that he thought the optimum weight was between 10 and 12lbs. The Pekingese's bowed forelegs were exceedingly difficult to breed out, and I find it interesting that it was in 1953, only one year after the Shih Tzu/Peke cross, that the word 'straight', with reference to the legs, was deleted from the Breed Standard. The current Standard reads: "as straight as possible."

The Peke cross had undoubtedly caused controversy, but the matter was not to end there, for the Lhakang kennel started to specialise in breeding 'tinies'. At an Annual General Meeting of the Shih Tzu Club there was a majority vote in favour of having the weight clause altered to "up to 18lbs, ideal weight, 9-16lbs." This, following hot on the heels of the unrest caused by the Peke cross, was enough to split both the Club and the breed in two. Those who objected to the breeding of miniatures thought that it would result in a toy breed, and this would bring associated whelping problems – thus far, the breed had been noted for its ease of whelping. Lady Brownrigg wrote to the Kennel Club begging them not to allow such a small size, but the KC did accept the revised Standard allowing 'tinies', though not miniatures. In consequence Lady Brownrigg requested that there should be a division into two size ranges, but this was not allowed for the breed was not numerically strong enough to warrant such a division. Weight classes were, however, put on at shows so that the smaller specimens might be accommodated, such classes being guaranteed by the club.

Mrs Longden set up a private club in 1956, with the aim of promoting the smaller size, and although application was made to the Kennel Club for it to have its own title, permission was not

Mrs Gay Widdrington with some of her Shih Tzu in 1960. These include (top left) Ch. Mayawong of Lhakang, (top right) Ch. Mao-Mao of Lhakang and (bottom right, facing) Ch. Tien Memsahib.

Photo courtesy G. Widdrington.

Ch. Whitethroat Chinese Gem (Ch. Jen-Kai-Ko of Lhakang – Whitethroat Mei-Ling). Bred and owned by Mrs Eunice Fox. Photo by Pearce, courtesy Mrs G. Widdrington.

granted. Owen Grindey, who was later to become Chairman of the new club, was instrumental in changing the aims to be: "to promote and protect the breed and preserve it on the right lines according to the Kennel Club Standard of 1958", in addition to which the same official Standard was to be used. This being so, the Kennel Club granted its permission and the Manchu Shih Tzu Club officially came into being.

As the 1960s progressed registrations rose steadily, as did exports abroad. Most exports went to the USA, but in that decade over a hundred Shih Tzu, many of which were not bred by established breeders, went to Japan where, today, the Shih Tzu has become the most popular breed. In England breed history was made in 1963 when Ch. Pan-Mao Chen of Antartica, owned by Ken and Betty Rawlings, won Best in Show at WELKS (West of England Ladies' Kennel Society). The 1960s also saw the first Shih Tzu of the smaller size gaining its crown, this was the black and white bitch, Ch. Tien Memsahib (Bimbo – Mu Ho), weighing ten pounds. She was bred by the late Thelma Morgan and owned by Mrs Widdrington. The breed moved steadily into the 1970s and in 1971 the Breed Standard was again altered to the wording: "10-18lbs, ideal 10-16lbs."

It is always difficult to know when the past ends and the present era begins. Clearly there are many dedicated breeders who, though no longer with us, bred lines which live on in the winning stock of today. I have detailed some of their achievements in a series of kennel cameos in the following chapter. Imports have also played a strong part in the development of the breed, and it is interesting to see how the Shih Tzu became established around the world.

AN EARLY IMPORT FROM NORWAY

Queen Maud of Norway brought one of Henrik Kauffmann and his wife's puppies back to England in 1933. This was for the Duchess of York, who was later to become Queen Elizabeth, and is now the Queen Mother. The dog, Choo Choo, was a son of the Kauffmanns' original pair imported from China, Aidze and Schander. A mating took place between Choo Choo and Lady Langman's Fu of Taishan and Lady Langman reared the litter in Yeoville. Mrs Bowes-Lyon was interested in Choo Choo's puppies and went to visit them with the result that one male puppy went to Princess Margaret, though Princess Elizabeth also spoke of him as her own. Li Ching Chao, from that same litter, features behind many pedigrees today.

IRELAND

It was Miss E. M. Hutchins who took the first Shih Tzu to Ireland in 1928, this was to her family home in Bantry, Co Cork. In the early days of the breed's history in Ireland, Miss Hutchins was the only exhibitor of the Shih Tzu, showing Tai Tai at the Irish Kennel Club's Show in 1933. Until the Second World War the breed was shown only in variety classes in Ireland, and although the breed was still exhibited following the war it did not grow numerically until the mid 1960s. Mrs Ruth Tennison was active with her Chasmu line, Mr and Mrs Winston Reynolds showed dogs from the Telota line and Frances Hickey's famous Lyre kennels showed and bred from Greenmoss dogs. By 1967 the Shih Tzu Club of Ireland had been founded and in 1970 Ireland had its first Shih Tzu Champion – Mrs P. Reynolds' Ir. Ch. Hollybough Tsing Hwa of Telota. In the same year the first Irish-bred Champion was made up – Ir. Ch. T'Wang of Lyre. Mrs Reynolds has had several other Irish Champions, and so has Mrs Frances Hickey whose Ir. Ch.

Taonan Boris of Lyre had numerous Best of Breed wins and was Ireland's top sire.

The Shih Tzu in Ireland has progressed steadily up to the present day, helped by the fact that Ireland's leading breeders keep in touch with each other through their active breed club, which regularly holds seminars and other functions. Since the Club's inception it has been policy to invite a breed specialist to judge the Club's Championship Show, and that specialist has then had the opportunity to talk to exhibitors when judging is complete. Influence from imported lines and the merging of various other lines has brought with it a great variety of colours in the breed in Ireland. Soundness has been a priority for breeders, and although faults have crept in from time to time they have generally been carefully bred out. It is felt that in Ireland the Shih Tzu are hardy dogs, well-muscled and with good bone and substance due, to a large extent, to the freedom of their life-style. Most owners in Ireland do not keep their dogs caged but allow them to run free. There have been problems of lack of coat and presentation in the past but these are now much improved, so much so that Irish dogs have been awarded Group and Best in Show wins at all breeds shows in recent years. Breeders recognise that it has been difficult to retain typical Shih Tzu hind action, but many breeders are now aware of this and are striving to improve it. With careful breeding size is now beginning to standardise, and as generations progress, the Irish Shih Tzu is continuing to improve.

NORWAY

Norway was the founder of Scandinavian Shih Tzu history. The first imports were two bitches and a dog, owned by the Danish Minister to China, Henrik Kauffmann, and his wife, who took them to Norway in 1932. The best of the three were Leidza (whelped 1928) who they thought to be "among the very best of her kind either in China or in Europe". She was a small, brown bitch, bought from an old palace eunuch, and said to be of palace stock. Aidze (also listed as Aidzo and whelped 1930) was a black and white male who was also small; it took the Kauffmanns a year and a half to find him. Although he was believed to be of good stock (on account of his size) they knew nothing of consequence about him. The third was Schander (listed as Schauder in USA and Norway and whelped 1931), a black and white bitch obtained a couple of years later and standing rather "higher from the ground" than the other two; for this reason she was thought not to be quite so good. The story of the acquisition of the Kauffmanns' first Shih Tzu is fascinating. Apparently, Mrs Kauffmann was walking along a street in Peking and saw some small long-haired dogs which were going to be burned in connection with a religious ceremony. She begged the Chinese to show mercy on the dogs and she managed to take one away with her. She was so enchanted with the dog that she resolved to find two more.

Mrs Kauffmann felt that none of Leidza's puppies was quite her equal, except perhaps "a little black and white one" which she sent to London. Another she sent to London was My Lord of Tibet, who had a white spot on his nose. Mrs Kauffmann had a Chinese 'amah' with her in Norway who had apparently learned a great deal about the Chinese standards for the breed and had imparted this knowledge to the Kauffmanns. Throughout the thirties the Shih Tzu was still registered in Norway as a Lhassa Terrier, and it was not until 1939 that the Norsk Kennel Club wrote to Lady Brownrigg asking what such dogs were called in England and requesting Breed Standards for the "Lhassa Terrier and the Shih Tzu." There was, it seems, a little confusion over the description of the jaw placement in the Kauffmanns' Shih Tzu. Mrs Kauffmann mentioned some puppies with a "slightly undershot jaw." Later though, in 1937 she wrote: "I must write

Nord. Ch. Lhakang Jolyon (Golden Plover of Lhakang – Honey-Bee of Lhakang). Foundation stud for the Boreas kennel, he is pictured with Major Bonne Hasle in Norway. Jolyon has sired fifteen Champions and is the grandsire of at least thirty-five others.

Photo courtesy Mrs G. Widdrington.

Int. N & S Ch. Spovens Little Sweet Success. Top winning Shih Tzu in Norway, 1991. Rune Ostby Hansen.

and explain that none of my dogs have receding lower jaws – what you call 'even' was what I called 'receding' because the lower teeth fit in behind the upper ones."

By June of 1936 the Kauffmanns had lost a bitch in whelp and had only one left, a honey-coloured bitch who was at least ten years old and so not expected to have any more puppies. The Kauffmanns and Brownriggs exchanged regular correspondence, and it seems clear that Mrs Kauffmann had great respect for Lady Brownrigg's opinions; Lady Brownrigg playing an important role in getting the breed registered as Shih Tzu in Norway. Mrs Else Grum, wife of the Danish Consul, was one of the first people to become fascinated by the Kauffmanns' Shih Tzu, remaining faithful to the breed for many years. Other pioneers of the breed in Norway include: Mrs Adele Heyerdahl (Flinthaugs), Mrs Asta Helliksen (Voksenlias) and Mr John Normann (Dux). Despite the length of time that the Shih Tzu has been in Norway there is still no breed club, but the breed is one of thirty-two represented by the Norwegian Miniature Dog Club, most of which have their own elected representative and working committee to take care of the breed's special needs and to promote its interests. In recent years annual registrations for the breed have averaged just under two hundred.

The so called 'Nordic Type', which was rather narrow and high on the leg, is now almost a thing of the past; the Shih Tzu in Norway is now generally lower to the ground and with a more powerful body. Over recent years imports have gone into the country primarily from the UK and from Sweden. One of the major reasons for this is that quarantine is avoided, although there is a month's 'Home Quarantine' for dogs coming in from the UK. In fact, there was only one import from the UK registered with the Norwegian Kennel Club during 1990. It is more difficult to ascertain the numbers being imported from Sweden because dogs are allowed to keep and to use their Swedish registration papers in Norway. Undoubtedly British breeding has contributed to the current strength of quality of the Shih Tzu in Norway, and all of 1990's 'Top Ten' Shih Tzu in Norway have ancestry in the UK, though five were bred in Norway, three in Sweden and two in the UK.

Before Major B. Hasle's Champion bitch, Lhakang Celandine went to Norway it was quite rare to see a solid gold with a black mask. Others have now been imported and the colour can be now be seen with greater frequency, though gold and white is still the predominant colour. Although Major Hasle does not breed frequently, he has, over the years, exported dogs to many different countries. Ch. Spovens Royal Revelation (Ch. Greenmoss Titfer-Tat – Ch. Spovens Gaina-Zi) was not only top-winning Shih Tzu in Norway in 1990, but also top-winning dog of all the miniature breeds. He was also at the top of the list in 1989. Int. Nordic and Swedish Ch. Spovens Little Sweet Success was the most successful Shih Tzu of 1991, having now amassed three Best in Show wins, seven awards for best in Group and eight CACIBs. Both Royal Revelation and Sweet Success were bred by Mrs Lillevor Lindberg in Sweden and are owned by Rune Egebakken and Ioannis Politis. In Norway there are currently over forty shows each year offering an opportunity for CCs to be gained in the breed. The Shih Tzu in Norway now appears to be of high quality, but as is common in so many countries and in so many breeds, bitches are generally considered to be stronger in quality and depth than dogs. The Norwegians consider that the breed has so far been free from hereditary defects.

DENMARK

It was in the early 1940s that Miss Astrid Jepperson set up her Bjornholms kennel of Shih Tzu, having purchased her foundation bitch, Mai Ling Tzu au Dux (also listed as ... Av Dux), from Mr Normann in Oslo, Norway. This bitch, the result of a brother/sister mating, came from Kauffmann stock, and the Bjornholms kennel went on to have much influence in Scandinavia, exporting a number of dogs to Sweden, including Bjornholms Pippi in 1953.

There are presently between one hundred and one hundred and fifty Shih Tzu registered in Denmark each year, but there is no club specifically for the breed. Instead the Shih Tzu comes under the auspices of a 'Common Club' for those breeds with no society of their own. Some fifty breeds are included, and around forty members are owners of Shih Tzu. On average there are twenty to thirty Shih Tzu entered at each show. Over the last few years the top winning exhibits within the breed have been Danish and Int. Ch. Gaya's Shu-San-Yen (1985 and 1986), Danish and Int. Ch. Gaya's Khe-Zu-Shan (1987, 1988 and 1989), Danish and Int. Ch. Gaya's Yin-Su-Zi-Wong (1990) and Danish Ch. Boreas Yangtze Year O'Yield, who claimed the title in 1991. Recently there have been many Shih Tzu imported to Denmark from Sweden, Norway, Finland, Germany, France and the UK.

SWEDEN

Norwegian-bred Flinthaugs Da-Wa, bred by Mrs T. Heyerdahl and owned by Baron Carl Leuhusen was the first Shih Tzu in Sweden, arriving in 1950. Mrs Anna Hauffman of the Shepherd kennel became the first Swedish breeder; she imported Lindewangens Choo-Li (Ch. Flinthaugs Wu-Hi – Bjorneholms Karma) from Mrs Gertrud Wedege in Denmark. Looking at a five generation pedigree, it is fascinating to note that Choo-Li was line-bred no fewer than seven times back to Aidze and Schander. Wu-Ling Fengsao (Eng. Ch. Shebo Tsemo of Lhakang – Looching of The Mynd), the other dog which joined the Shepherd kennel with Choo-Li, was also line-bred back to these two dogs, through Choo-Choo. In the early history of the breed in Sweden, Mrs Maria Lindeberg's Av Brogyllen kennel started a breeding programme from Flinthaugs Lung-Toy and Flinthaugs Li-Tzu, imported from Norway. By 1953 Bjorneholms Pippi had arrived from Denmark and he, along with other stock from the same kennel and the English-bred Ch Fu-Ling of Clytsvale, founded Mr and Mrs Carl-Olof Jungefeldt's kennel under the prefix Jungfaltet. The influence of these breeding lines has not only been important in Sweden but useful exports were also made both to the continent and to the USA. In 1955 Ch. Bjornholms Pippi was the first Shih Tzu to win Best in Show at an all breeds show. The Beldam, Marina, Lundehill, Bymarken, Lyckobringaren and Anibes kennels soon followed, along with others, all contributing to the popularity of the breed in Sweden. In general, the early Shih Tzu are reputed to have been very sound, with good movement and they had dark pigmentation and good bites.

Judges have officiated in Sweden from all over the world, and the Shih Tzu in this country clearly have a high reputation for quality and consistency of type, continuing Pippi's mark in history by winning Best in Show awards. The majority of imports have gone into Sweden from the UK with some also from Finland and Norway. These, mixed with Scandinavian lines, have allowed some necessary breed points to be improved, with both soundness and good temperament being passed down through the generations. Annual registrations for the breed in Sweden currently run at around six hundred, and, unlike the UK, the breed is part of the Toy Group, in which there are only three breeds with higher registration figures. The Swedish Shih Tzu Society was founded in 1969 and by the close of that year had two hundred and twenty-five

Mrs Gay Widdrington judging in Sweden in 1980. Pictured (left) is Anita Berggren's Swed. GB and Int. Ch. Bellakerne Suki-Sue, handled by Paul Stanton and (right) Int. Ch. Kurt's Boy of Lansu.

Photo courtesy Mr and Mrs T. Richardson.

members. In Sweden breed specialist judges frequently officiate at breed club shows, while all-rounders are more usually to be found in the centre of the ring at general shows, giving that important cross-section of viewpoints so vital for any breed.

FINLAND

Mrs Irja Kunnari introduced the breed to Finland in 1955: the first imports were Shepherds Yen-Psung and Shepherds Hien Kiang, both bred by Anne Haufmann in Sweden. The first Finnish-born Shih Tzu litter was whelped at Mr Antti Seppala's Capella kennel in 1961. Since then there have been many high quality Shih Tzu bred in this country. Mrs Heidi Backlund (Baron-sonit) was another of the early pioneers. There are no 'commercial' Shih Tzu kennels for the breed in Finland and registrations average only around one hundred dogs per year. This is a situation which the Finnish breeders would like to see remain, for they find it "heart-breaking" that the breed has risen so rapidly in the popularity stakes in so many other countries. However, the small numbers bred in Finland present a challenge to breeders to maintain quality, due to the inevitable dangers of a small gene pool. For this reason they have always regarded it as important to avoid what they call 'matador breeding' of one stud dog. Some new blood has been imported from abroad and breeders recognise that this will also be necessary in the future. Since the 1970s most of that new blood has been from the UK, either by direct imports or from English blood imported via Norwegian and Swedish stock. The Finnish people believe that they have obtained most of what they describe as the 'classical' English lines.

Many breed specialists have judged in Finland and they have appreciated the good bone and bodies of the show stock. They have also been well satisfied with the breed's round skulls, square muzzles and open nostrils. In recent years toplines, fronts and tails have been substantially improved, along with coat texture and the art of presentation. All colours are

UK SF Ch. Lhakang Cassius (Tor Ra Lon – Cherubim of Lhakang). Cassius went to Finland after gaining his English title, sire of Ch. Jem-Gem Choir Angel, he was bred by Mrs G. Widdrington and owned by Mrs I. Brooker and then Miss E. Verlander.
Photo courtesy Mrs G. Widdrington.

Ch. Jem-Gem Choir Angel (UK SF Ch. Lhakang Cassius – SF Ch. Jem-Gem Cho-Ko-Bud). Bred and owned by Ritva Nissila of Finland, he was world winner at the World Show in Dortmund, 1991.

Photo courtesy Mrs G. Widdrington.

represented in the breed in Finland with, I understand, the exception of the pure black and white. In 1971 the Finnish Shih Tzu Club was established and not only does it arrange shows and gatherings but also issues breed magazines and year books. The club's Breeding Council collects statistics on health problems in the breed and gives advice and information to breeders. Most representatives of the breed are located in the southern and western parts of the country and, while it is acknowledged that breed type varies somewhat in the northern parts of Finland, the Shih Tzu is undoubtedly well established. Finnish breeders try to avoid all exaggerations, keeping the breed healthy and true to type. In Eija Verlander's words: "We must remember that people come and go, but the breed stays there after us."

GERMANY

The first Shih Tzu kennel was founded in Germany in 1960, and this was Mrs Erika Geusendam's Kennel von Tschomo-Lungma in Lubeck. The first import was Bjornholms Ling-Fu, but sadly she died in whelp during 1961. Mrs Geusendam produced her first litter of three puppies from Int. Ch. Bjornholms Pif and Int. Ch. Bjornholms Ting-a-Ling. She went on to breed over eighty Champions, including twenty-three International Champions, and others have carried titles in Austria, Belgium, Canada, the former Soviet Union, Germany, Denmark, France, Holland, Italy, Luxembourg, Monaco, Spain, Switzerland and the USA. Stock from this kennel has also been responsible for nine World Winner titles. One of the exports to the USA was Ch. Tangra vom Tschomo-Lungma, who went out in whelp to Bjornholms Pif. The resulting litter produced the famous US and Can. Ch. Chumulari Ying-Ying, owned by Rev Easton. Mrs Geussendam tried to breed only from stock which went back to the original Scandinavian imports, but in order to bring in fresh blood she imported three dogs and a bitch from a litter bred especially by Mrs Gay Widdrington without any of the Peke-cross blood. In 1987 she deviated from her previous personal rule and brought in a dog bred by Anita Bergren, Anibes Shot In The Dark (Ch. Whitethroat Jarvis – Ch. Yrings No Stuffed Toi For Anibes). Ch. Faran v. Tschomo-Lungma, whelped in 1977, was one of the most highly successful dogs from this kennel. He was World Winner in 1979 and 1981 and gained his Championship titles in Germany, Belgium, Denmark and Holland. Faran's dam, Ch. Naga v. Tschomo-Lungma, produced three further International Champions.

In 1968 Mrs Ruth Vorderstemann founded her Heydpark kennel, now in the hands of Mrs Carola Vorderstemann. Six Champions have been bred out of this kennel, which in 1982 imported Ban-Zai's Shu-Fu-Yen-Ku from Denmark, who was to gain a German Championship title. Two Champions have been bred in the Lin-Pearl kennel, set up by Linda Reinelt-Gebauer in 1975. She imported two dogs from Britain, Keytor Sweet Jasmin, bred by Susan and Ellen Johnson and Puttin On The Top Hat, bred by the Dolphin/Bergren partnership. The Johnson partnership also provided Keytor Marissa, the foundation bitch for Mrs Ruth Kruss' Kennel Zum Fledermausturmchen, which has produced three Champions since its foundation in 1979. The eighties saw the foundation of Jens Niderjasass' Jenshu and Simone Menne's Shente kennels, both of which have produced Champion stock.

In the early stages of its history in Germany the Shih Tzu was one of about a dozen small breeds looked after by the Verband Deutscher Kleinhundezuchter e V, but in 1980 The Int. Shih Tzu Club e V was founded by Mrs Linda Reinelt-Gebauer, who had previously been a successful breeder of Pekingese and thought that the Shih Tzu deserved greater popularity. In 1981 there were only twelve Shih Tzu registered with the club, but by 1989 the figure had risen to one hundred and eighty-eight. Stock in Germany was imported primarily from the UK and from Denmark, but Shih Tzu were also imported from Belgium, the former Soviet Union, France, Sweden, USA and the Netherlands. Since 1986 the Int. Shih Tzu Club has held a competition for the top-winning Shih Tzu, and in its first five years this was won by Ger., VDH, Int. Ch. Aramis von Shen-Te (br./owner Simone Menns, Germany); Ger., VDH, Danish, Int. Ch. Greenmoss Song Of Bee (br. J. & A. Leadbitter, UK); Ger., VDH, Austrian, Swiss, Lux., Int. Ch. Kelemar Linze-Lu (br. M. & R. Brannick, UK); Danish, Ger., VDH, Int. Ch. Boreas Little Apollo (br. B. Hasle, Norway) and Ger., VDH, Danish Ch. Lin-Pearl's Sing A Song (br./owner L. Reinelt-Gebaur, Germany).

NETHERLANDS

During the 1960s the leading breeder of Shih Tzu in the Netherlands was Mrs Eta Pauptit, who had made a careful study of the breed, both in the Scandinavian countries and in Britain, before founding her Oranje Manege kennels which were to become renowned throughout the world. Int. and Dutch Ch. Hang Shu v.d Oranje Manege has been perhaps the most famous of her stud dogs. Now there is a specialist breed society for the Shih Tzu in the Netherlands.

CZECHOSLOVAKIA

Czechoslovakia's first Shih Tzu arrived in the country in 1980, imports coming from Germany, Italy, Belgium and Austria. Most of these were bitches but later imports, including dogs, came in from Holland, Sweden and the USA. The first Shih Tzu litter was born in Czechoslovakia in 1980, and in November 1983 the Shih Tzu Breeders' Club was founded; current membership is now over two hundred. Since the breed's introduction to the country around two thousand Shih Tzu have been registered in the 'breed book' of which over three hundred have been 'admitted for breeding' The average litter size has been calculated to be between three and five puppies. The principal colours to be found in the breed in Czechoslovakia are gold and white, black and white, black masked gold and white, and there are a few blacks, silvers and golds with black masks.

Until 1989 it was almost impossible for breeders from Czechoslovakia to travel abroad and, although the situation has now improved, financial problems hinder breeding programmes, and suitable individuals to which they can line-breed are limited. The Czechoslovak breeders feel that they need a significant import of high quality stock from the UK. They believe that as the Shih Tzu has been in this country for so long, stock is "of the highest quality". There are over forty regional exhibitions each year where Shih Tzu are scheduled, plus two national and two international exhibitions. The club holds three shows each year, each with CAC standing, and it is encouraging to know that at the 1990 World Show there were twenty-five exhibits from Czechoslovakia, many of which competed successfully against breed representatives from other countries.

FRANCE

The Countess d'Anjou bred Shih Tzu in China in Peking long before the Chinese revolution, and it was she who introduced the breed to France in 1950 and wrote the first French Standard for the breed. The Standard she wrote received the approval of the Ambassador of France and of Paraguay. He had spent many years in China and had owned a number of 'Tibetan Lion Dogs' which he also judged at shows in Peking. The Countess said that in Peking the breed was divided into two sizes, under and over 12lbs, each being judged separately. However, she most definitely felt that the breed should be under 12lbs and was quite adamant that there were none of the larger dogs in the Imperial Palace. Much of the Countess' information about the breed in China had come from the Princess Der Ling, who was in a position to know what the Palace dogs were actually like.

During the 1970s people began to show a definite interest in the Shih Tzu in France, but it was not until the 1980s that the breed became really popular. Currently there are around two thousand Shih Tzu puppies registered each year, and breeders acknowledge that in France there are what they call the 'English type, with a strong body and big head' and 'the American type, smaller than the English.' The Club des Chiens Tibetains de France (CCTF) asks that breeders, whatever their preference, aim to produce "beautiful and good dogs with the lovely Shih Tzu temperament and to respect the official Breed Standard."

SWITZERLAND

The Schweizerischer Zwerghunde Club (SZC) is a club for all Utility and Toy breeds which do not have their own breed club, and caters for twenty-two breeds, including the Shih Tzu. Although it cannot be ascertained that it was actually the first Shih Tzu in Switzerland, the first registration for the breed was made in 1956: a bitch by the name of Di Ji Anjou, imported from the Countess d'Anjou in France and owned by E. Franioli. As no registrations for offspring can be traced it would appear that this bitch was never bred from. There was another registration in 1963, defined as "small Tibet Terrier, Lhasa Apso, Shih Tzu" but as there seem to be no bloodlines to the Shih Tzu it has been assumed in Switzerland that this was most probably a Tibetan Terrier.

It was in 1967 that Mrs Trudy Brandenberg of the Shantung kennel imported Padma v. Tschomo-Lungma (Bjorneholms Bhadro – Bjornholms Ting-a-Ling) from Mrs Geusendam in Germany. In the same year Mrs L. Tanner imported a dog, Maudee's Dauphin, from Norway but as he was not registered as a stud it is presumed that he was kept purely as a pet. The following year, in October, Mrs Brandenberg bred Switzerland's first litter of Shih Tzu, producing two dogs and two bitches out of Padma v. Tschomo-Lungma who was mated in Holland to Hang-Shu v.d. Orange Manege, belonging to Mrs Edith Popti. That same year Mrs Brandenberg imported two more Shih Tzu and in 1969 she bred her second litter. Mrs Doris Meier was a well-known breeder of Boston Terriers and Pekingese, and in 1970 she imported from England Corin of Bracewell (Pei Ying Of Greenmoss – Tonia of Bracewell) and Golden Empress of Elfann (Golden Peregrine Of Elfann – Fire Fly Of Lhakang). This pair was mated, and produced the first Shih Tzu litter for the Arcadia kennel in 1971. The two dogs imported from Ireland were litter brother and sister, Gina Dina and Royal Relief, but there is no confirmation as to whether or not these dogs were bred from as there are no recorded registrations. People are now taking notice of and admiring the Shih Tzu in Switzerland and a lively interest is shown in the breed.

AUSTRALIA

In 1954 Mr and Mrs Dobson (Wawnhill) took three British Shih Tzu to their new home in New South Wales. These were Pei Ho of Taishan, a black and white male, Wen Chi Of Lhakang, a chestnut and white puppy dog, and Chloe of Elfann, a black bitch. The first litter, sired by Pei Ho, was born in quarantine and the resulting offspring were to find themselves in various different Australian States. Mrs Avery and Mrs Gwen Teele (Geltree) were two of the earliest Shih Tzu breeders in Australia, and they have done much for the breed. Many British Shih Tzu have been exported to Australia and, in turn, Australia has exported the breed to many different countries including Japan, Malaysia, Singapore and Sweden. Although in the early days there was a great variation in type the breed has become much more uniform over the years.

UNITED STATES OF AMERICA

We have already discussed the confusion which arose due to the incorrect registration of the Shih Tzu when it first arrived the USA, but the UK Pekingese-Shih Tzu cross also had an important bearing on the progress of the breed. In the UK the progeny of the third filial generation cross was registered as Shih Tzu with the English Kennel Club, but in the USA a further three generations had to be bred from the initial cross before pure-bred registration were accepted. It was not until 1955 that the Shih Tzu began to receive status in the United States. By then a group of enthusiastic breeders were able to offer sufficient proof of nationwide interest in the breed for it to be accepted as one of thirteen breeds which could be exhibited in the miscellaneous class. The first recorded appearance of the Shih Tzu in public came at the Philadelphia Show in 1957.

By 1960 the Texas Shih Tzu Society and the Shih Tzu Club of America had been formed and a Mr Curtis was also active in endeavouring to register his Shih Tzu with the AKC. Eventually the two clubs combined, though Mr Curtis did not join that merger. Thus the American Shih Tzu Club was formed in 1963 and, in accordance with AKC rules, a stud book was maintained, recording in July of that year three hundred and sixty-nine Shih Tzu of American and foreign breeding. The first match show for the breed took place in 1964. Sponsored by the Penn-Ohio Shih Tzu Club, it was held at Ingrid Coleman's home in Pennsylvania, and fifty-one of the country's Shih Tzu were entered under judge Mrs Eunice Clark of Ohio. The overall winner was Margaret Easton's Si-Kiang Tashi, an all black, bred by Mrs Colwell whose Swedish import, Fr. Ch. Jungfeltets Jung Wu, took the best opposite sex award. Both were descended from Scandinavian Ch. Bjornholm Wu-Ling. By now the breed was beginning to become fashionable and a handful of early dedicated breeders did much to promote the breed. A second Match took place the following year and this was judged by the UK's Audrey Fowler. On March 16th, 1969, the AKC finally allowed the breed registration in its Stud Book, by which time there were around three thousand dogs and bitches eligible for registration. It is interesting to note that between 1960 and 1969 there were six hundred and forty-two imports from the UK. Five months later the Shih Tzu was able to compete for Championship points and on that very first day a Shih Tzu won a Best in Show award in the East and elsewhere two others won their Toy Groups. The Best in Show winner on this historic occasion was Rev and Mrs D Allan-Easton's three-year-old Canadian Ch. Chumulari Ying Ying and the award came under judge James Trullinger at the New Brunswick Kennel Club Show at Metuchen, New Jersey. The breed judge was Alva

Rosenberg and the total entry at the show was 970 dogs. Also reaching great heights on that day was sire of the above, Mary Wood's and Norman Patton's Int. Ch. Bjornholmes Pif, winner of the Toy Group at Corn Belt Kennel Club. In Oregon Jean Gadsbury's Lakoya Princess Tanya Shu, a one-year-old grand-daughter of Pif, won the Group there. Thus these great awards were won by three consecutive generations.

It was Bjornholmes Pif who was to become the breed's first Champion in the USA, winning the necessary fifteen Championship points in just thirteen days! He had been imported from Denmark the previous year, when he had already gained his title in five different countries. In the following year he tied for the award of 'Top Producing Toy Sire'. The first bitch to gain her title in the USA was a daughter of the winner of that very first Match in 1964. This was Ch. Chumulari Hih-Hih, who also managed to gain her points in thirteen days. She was very soon to be joined by Ch. Lakoya Princess Tanya Shu, who gained her crown in the space of twenty-seven days. In that year, of the ninety-three Shih Tzu who gained their Championship titles more than half were sired by only eight dogs, each of these having sired at least three Champion offspring. In 1973 at Portland, Oregon, there was the first opportunity for Championship points to be gained at a Specialty show. Despite its slow start, due to a combination of complex issues, undoubtedly the Shih Tzu went on to gain rapid popularity in the USA, where it continues to have high status in the dog showing world.

SOME PIONEERS IN AMERICA

Ingrid Colwell (affix: Si-Kiang), born in Sweden, was the daughter of the Swedish Shih Tzu breeder, Ingrid Engstrom (affix: Pukedals). She bought her first Shih Tzu bitch in Germany in 1958 while her husband was stationed in Germany. Her interest in the breed grew and by the time she moved to the USA in 1960 she had four Shih Tzu which were to form her foundation stock, and these were soon to be joined by an import, Jungfaltets Wu-Pu. Ingrid Colwell was clearly a most dedicated and enthusiastic breeder, always anxious to impart her knowledge to others. How sad it was that she died tragically as a result of fire in January of 1968.

The 'Mariljac' partnership of **Mary and Jack Woods** got their first Shih Tzu from the UK in 1959, and they played an important part in forming the American Shih Tzu Club. Following the death of Mr Wood, Mrs Wood continued breeding under the same affix with **Norman Patton,** who was known for his 'Dragonwyck' affix. Among his many top wining Shih Tzu is the famous Ch. Dragonwyck The Great Gatsby. Encore Chopsticks, owned by **Bill and Joan Kibler** (affix: Taramount), had an exceptional show career, winning the Shih Tzu Club's 'Specialty' for six consecutive years against stiff competition. He had been retired by the time the breed was officially recognised in 1969 but was the sire of no fewer than fourteen Champions and has firmly imprinted his mark on the breed. It was the Kiblers who bred what seems to have been the first Swedish/English litter in the USA in 1961 from Encore Lovely Lady (of English stock) and La Mi Ting Ling (Swedish bred). It is relevant to mention that much of the Kiblers' stock incorporates the name 'Encore' but the AKC refused the registration of this word as an affix.

The Chumulari affix is owned by **the Reverend D. Allan Easton** and his wife, **Margaret**. It was Rev Easton who actually saw what are believed to have been the last two Shih Tzu to leave Peking, these having been bred by Alfred Koehn and purchased by the British Consul. It was not until 1961 that the Eastons managed to buy their first Shih Tzu; this was Si-Kiang's Tashi who won that first ever Shih Tzu Match in 1964. In addition, they imported Wei-Honey Gold of

Am. Ch. Jungfaltets Jung-Wu owned by Ingrid Colwell who helped to establish the breed in the USA. Bred by Asrid Jeppesen of Denmark, Jung-Wu is a typical Scandinavian type Shih Tzu and descends from three Chinese imports.
Photo courtesy Mrs G. Widdrington.

Elfann and Jemima of Lhakang from England and later Swiss and Czechoslovak Ch. Tangra v Tschomo Lungma, from Germany. The latter, who went on to become a Canadian Champion, was already in whelp on her arrival in the United States and produced the famous Am. Can. Ch. Chumulari Ying Ying, sire of at least twenty-nine Champions. **Margaret Edel** (affix: Mar-Del) helped in that early struggle for breed recognition and, having acquired her first stock from Ingrid Colwell, she went on to breed one of the country's top producers, Ch. Mar-Del's Ring-A-Ding-Ding. Another who worked towards recognition of the breed in those early years was **Andy Hickok Warner** (affix: Rosemar), who also obtained her first Shih Tzu from Ingrid Colwell, as did **Pat Semones Durham** (affix: Pa-Sha and Si-Kiang). Some of Ingrid's Shih Tzu also came into her ownership following the tragedy of the fire.

As the sixties and seventies progressed more and more enthusiasts steadily joined the ranks of dedicated Shih Tzu breeders in America, among them Florence and Louis Sanfilippo (affix: Char-Nick). Their first home-bred Champion was Ch. Char-Nick's Sam Chu, to be followed by many others including the highly successful Ch. Char-Nick's I Gotcha. Other relatively early pioneers worthy of note are Dr and Mrs J. Wesley Edel (afix: Emperor), Joan Cowie (affix: Nanjo) and Rae Eckes (affix: House of Wu) and, naturally, there are many others but in a country as large as the USA, and with the Shih Tzu reaching high in the popularity stakes, it would simply not be possible to mention everyone.

AMERICAN BLOODLINES IN THE UK

Although a dog from Canada had previously come into Britain's Keytor kennels, the first *all* American Shih Tzu to be imported to Great Britain by a show kennel were Dragonfire's Scarlet O'Hara, a deep red and white bitch, sired by the famous Ch. Dragonfire's Red Raider out of Dragonfire's Great Dracaena, and Dragonfire's All American Boy, who came to Michael and

Am. Ch. Dragonfire's Red Raider ROM. Multiple Group winner, owned by Mrs P. Hogg (Dragonfire's).

Dragonfire's All American Boy, bred in the USA by Mrs Hogg, he was imported to the UK by Michael and Dee Harper. His sire is Am. Ch. Dragonfire's Red Raider and his dam is Am. Ch. Dragonfire's Dang Sai Dickens.
Photo by Carol Ann Johnson.

Ten-month-old Harropine Columbus, a son of US import Dragonfire's All American Boy out of Harropine Atlantic Star. *Photo by Carol Ann Johnson.*

Dee Harper of the well known Harropine affix. American Boy, winner of one CC in the UK, is a bright, clear gold and white male of great presence, again by Ch. Dragonfire's Red Raider, his dam is Ch. Dragonfire's Dang Sai Dickens. Both of these Shih Tzu come from Mrs Peggy Hogg in Illinois, USA, owner of the famous Dragonfire's affix. Apart from being a highly successful American breeder and exhibitor, she is also well known for her expert handling, especially of the very famous US Ch. Dragonwyck The Great Gatsby, bred by Norman Patton. This dog was a multiple winner and features behind most of the Dragonfire's latest Champions. The superb rich chestnut colour, evident in so many of the Dragonfire's dogs is a colour which would be desirable in the UK. A few of the famous dogs and bitches in American Boy's ancestry are Ch. Dragonfire's Red Raider ROM, Ch. Dragonwyck The Great Gatsby, Ch. Dragonfire's I'm Mahalia and Ch. Dragonfire's Dang Sai Angie Dickens. Michael Harper feels that the interesting part about importing this particular line was to introduce the exceptionally strong, clear colours and excellent front assembly, while retaining the correct size of the Shih Tzu and tail placement. Heads were slightly different, but correct, and mixed well into Harropine lines producing a satisfying blend. The colours have been most exciting, especially some wonderful black and whites, red and whites and gold and whites. The coat is voluminous and its texture is strong. The results, so far, have been extremely encouraging.

Am. Ch. Di Ho Rupert T. Bear was imported to the UK when his owner, Mrs Jane Couch came to England in 1987. 'Rupert' is just one of the famous 'Bears' from the Winward line of the late Mimi Bump. Rupert's grandsire, Ch. Winwards Wheeler Dealer, mated to Lou Wan Afternoon Delight, produced both Rupert's sire, Mandalays Blockbuster and the famous Ch. Winwards

Ch. Snaefells Limited Edition and his sister Snaefells Licks and Kisses, sired by Am. Ch. Di Ho Rupert T. Bear out of Snaefells Irma La Douce. Owned by Audrey Dadds.

Free Wheeler. Of equal importance was the dam's line in which there were dogs of similar, excellent quality. The late Helen Strom, who was a breeder held in high regard in America, bred Rupert out of Din Ho Oriental Poppy, his sire being the well known Ch. Ming Toi P. V. Spunky, by the famous Ch. Parquins Pretty Boy Floyd and out of the bitch Din Ho Wan Shih Poppy, both top producers. The English import on this line was Talifu Bobby Dazzler, bred by Kitty Boot, and coming from similar lines to Mrs Audrey Dadds' own stock.

Mrs Dadds considers that these American breeders had bred for soundness of quality and type rather than glamour, and that their dogs were renowned for their lovely, large heads and well constructed bodies which, in consequence gave the true Shih Tzu action. She felt them to be good, honest Shih Tzu as she knew them, but with that "something extra". She needed an outcross and decided that these dogs had what she had bred for over the years, though without using an outcross some of the features would be difficult to retain. This line was smaller in type, but that did not worry her greatly. There was another quality which she recognised and needed, something which she was aware of in so many of the American dogs – that undefinable "extra", that "look at me", so essential in the show ring. Coupled with that, she found them very strong in their good driving action, level backs and good front assembly, giving a correctly set on head. These were qualities which Audrey Dadds did not wish to lose. She feels that her choice proved to be correct, for not only did she retain what she wanted, she brought in the "extra" as well. Both the dog and the bitch from the first litter to Snaefells Irma La Douce proved a success.

The dog from this litter, Ch. Snaefells Limited Edition, was the first Shih Tzu from American bloodlines to become a Champion in the UK. He had been used at very limited stud but his progeny have proved themselves and are winning in the ring. Mrs Dadds feels that Limited Edition has been able to put across that indefinable "something" which is needed, and which he gained from his American line. With puppies from his first litter he won both a breed club and an all-breed progeny class at Championship level. Sister to Limited Edition, Snaefells Licks and Kisses has also won well, though withdrawn from the ring for almost a year due to her litter. She, too, has imparted her "extra something" to her puppies. The mating to Rupert has been repeated and the same qualities have again come through.

Audrey Dadds is strongly of the opinion that careful breeding of mixed lines is needed, but that we must recognise that there will inevitably be bad as well as good. It is just as essential to know any undesirable faults which may be brought in from mixing lines as it is to know the good points. Wise breeders will learn from this and make full use of the good qualities. This, though, will not happen in one generation. Breeding is a long term project and breeders must recognise that any new lines can bring in both desirable and undesirable qualities. Good breeders will aim to retain the good and breed out the bad. That is where the joy of breeding comes in.

CANADA

In Canada the earliest pioneers of the breed were Mr and Mrs Patrick Morgan (Chouette) and Miss Margaret Torrible (Mrs Burbank) of Kokonor fame. As in the USA there was confusion over the name of the breed in the early years of its history on this continent, the names Tibetan Terrier and Lhassa Terrier both adding to the dilemma. Discussion took place between breeders in Canada and the Shih Tzu Club of England with regard to the eventual registration of Canadian Shih Tzu. A Shih Tzu from England went to the Morgans' Chouette kennel in 1935 and three came to England from that kennel in 1938, though sadly only one survived. This was Tashi of Chouette who played an important role in strengthening English lines. Another dog in the Chouette kennel was Hooza who came from Peking and Mingk (a 'pepper and white') went to the same kennel from Czechoslovakia. Jeff Carrique, founder of the Carrimount line, has been a highly successful breeder in Canada and during the 1970s one of the most successful Champions was Messrs Frederico and Guzzi's Ch. Choo Lang of Telota.

Chapter Four

KENNEL CAMEOS

ANTARTICA: Kenneth Rawlings and his late wife, Betty, became involved with Shih Tzu in 1950, initially with Perky Ching Of The Mynd, and they went on to breed and to campaign a great many Champions during their many years of involvement with the breed. Their Ch. Shebo Tsemo Of Lhakang, bred by Mrs Widdrington in 1948, was a strong influence in the Antartica kennel producing two Champion offspring in Ch. Shu-ssa of Mitchelcombe, a bitch, and Ch. Yi Ting Mo of Antartica, a dog who was to head a long line of Champions. Ch Chi-Ma-Che of Antartica, bred by Mrs Longden, sired two Champions, Chan Shih of Darite and Kuang Kuang of Antartica, both bred by Mr and Mrs Rawlings. Ch. Pan Wao Chen of Antartica, bred by Mrs St John Gore in 1960, went Best in Show at WELKS in 1963. The Rawlings were the owners of the breed's record holder until 1988; Ch. Kuire Hermes of Antartica amassed a total of twenty-seven CCs. In 1987 Ch. Harropine Chaka Khan at Antartica won the Utility Group at Crufts.

BELLAKERNE: Tom and Sheila Richardson first became involved with the breed in 1965 and their first Champion, Patsy Do of Hyning, gained her title in 1974, winning a total of twelve CCs. Two more Champions, this time owner-bred, followed in 1978. These were Ch. & In. Ch. Bellakerne Suki Sue, who was Top Toy in Sweden for three years, and Ch. Bellakerne Zippity Do who, like Patsy Do, amassed twelve CCs. Ch. Bellakerne Inca Do was soon to follow and then Champions Bellakerne Melisa Do and Pagan Do. Another champion carrying the Bellakerne prefix was Bellakerne Zoe-Do, owned by the late Thelma Morgan.

Tom and Sheila Richardson first awarded CCs in 1981 and 1982 respectively, and the highlight of Tom's judging career in the breed was his appointment to judge the parent club's Championship show. Tom and Sheila have both been active members of the Manchu Shih Tzu Society and Tom is currently Chairman of the Society.

Ch. Patsy Do of Hyning (Ch. Ching Ling of Greenmoss – Lindy Lou of Hyning).

Ch. Bellakerne Inca Do (Hyning Yes Sir – Ch. Patsy Do of Hyning).

Ch. Bellakerne Zoe Do (Ch. Greenmoss Chinki's Fling – Ch. Patsy Do of Hyning). Bred by Tom and Sheila Richardson, owned by T. Morgan and G. Dolphin.

Ch. Bellakerne Pagan Do (Bellakerne Brady of Erddig – Samatha of Bellakerne).

CHELHAMA: Mrs Valerie Goodwin, Hon Secretary of the Manchu Shih Tzu Society, first became connected with the breed in 1975 and made up her first Champion, Ch. Queensfield Tutsi Wong of Chelhama, in 1981. Three other Champions followed: Ch. Chelhama Ajax Olympus, Ch. Chelhama Pericles and, in 1991, Ch. Magique Magpie of Chelhama. Mrs Goodwin has awarded Challenge Certificates in the breed since 1988 and has judged in Eire, Germany and in Sweden.

CROWVALLEY: Lesley Williams and his late wife, Stephanie, began breeding under the Crowvalley affix twenty-two years ago. Betty Taylor, who had bred under the Boufalls affix, married Lesley and went into partnership with the Crowvalley kennel six years ago. Ch. Crowvalley Tweedledum, a Group winner, won sixteen CCs, all under different judges except for one, the only repeat being at Crufts, where he twice won Reserve Best in Group, in 1977 and 1980. Tweedledum was also the first Welsh Shih Tzu Champion and the first of the breed to become a Veteran Stakes winner. 1977 was an especially good year for this kennel for Ch. Crowvalley Poseidon also took Reserve in the Utility Group at Doncaster. Ten Championship title holders have come from Crowvalley, including Ch. Delridge Golden Gemini, who was owned in partnership with Mrs Eileen Wilson and had a Reserve Group win at Blackpool. Another, Ch. Boufalls The Brigadier At Crowvalley, was bred by Betty before she joined the Crowvalley partnership.

Several Crowvalley dogs have gone abroad: Ch. Poseidon went to Brazil where he became a Grand International Champion, Crowvalley Minerva, with two CCs from the UK, went to Australia where she gained her Australian title, as did Aust. Ch. Crowvalley Shergar. Ch. Crowvalley Peter Pan also gained his title in New Zealand; in France Crowvalley Delphie became an International Champion as did the delightfully named Boufalls Willy Wumpkin.

Ch. Chelhama Ajax Olympus (Ch. Dominic of Telota – Ch. Queensfield Tutsi Wong of Chelhama).

Pearce.

Ch. Chelhama Pericles (Ch. Chelhama Ajax Olympus – Chelhama Persephone).

Ch. Magique Magpie of Chelhama (Huxlor King of Glory at Chelhama – Leithill Lucinda).

*Ch. Crowvalley
Tweedledum (Elfann
Golden Sunrise of
Tricina – Crowvalley
Yameeto).*
Lionel Young.

*Ch. & Grand Int. Ch.
Crowvalley Poseiden
(Ch. Crowvalley
Tweedledum – Aust.
Ch. Crowvalley
Minerva).
Lionel Young.*

*Ch. Crowvalley
Pegasus (Ch. &
Grand Int. Ch.
Crowvalley
Poseiden
– Tricina Kay).*

*Ch. & Aust. Ch.
Delridge Golden
Gemini at
Crowvalley (Ch.
Crowvalley Pegasus
– Delridge Kwan
Yin).*

*Ch. & NZ Ch.
Claropie Peter Pan
at Crowvalley (Ch.
Crowvalley Pegasus
– Claropie Pandie).
Lionel Young.*

*Ch. Crowvalley
Anniversary (Ch.
Crowvalley Pegasus
– Rosayleen
Minstral).
          Lionel Young.*

*Ch. Darrralls Felicity
(Ch. Ya Tung of
Antartica – Ch.
Khumar Cina Silk of
Darralls).*

Pearce.

*Ch. Darralls China
Snapdragon (Ch.
Crowvalley Pegasus
– Ch. Khumar China
Silk of Darralls).*

J. S. Gurney.

Both Lesley and Betty Williams feel that the Shih Tzu is losing its balance and arrogance because people are more interested in mouths and coats. They have also noticed too few representatives of the breed with typical 'tea-pot handle' tails.

DARRALLS: Dorothy Gurney became interested in the breed in the early 1960s and her first Shih Tzu, Darralls Kumar of Greenmoss, born in 1965, was to become the grandsire of two Champions in the Darralls household. Ch. Kumar China Silk of Darralls, bred by June Edwards in 1973, was the dam of Ch. Darralls Felicity and her brother Fidelio who was sire of Ch. Boufalls The Brigadier. Fidelio and his siblings, Darralls China Snapdragon and Darralls Celestial Silk of Koonim, were all successful in the Championship Show rings.

Partly due to business commitments and also due to her involvement with Afghan Hounds, Dorothy has only ever kept a small number of Shih Tzu and has bred only the occasional litter. Despite this, home-bred Ch. Darralls Felicity, whelped in 1977, gained her title in 1980 and was the top winning Shih Tzu that year, having won eight CCs. She was retired at the end of that very same year at the tender age of three and a half years. Sadly she did not produce a litter.

From a purely personal point of view, my own interest in the Shih Tzu was greatly strengthened from watching Felicity grow up during the late 1970s. I am greatly indebted to her for transforming a mere interest into a love of and fascination for the breed.

Dorothy Gurney first awarded Challenge Certificates in the breed in 1978 since when she has regularly judged the breed in Britain and has also officiated in Belgium, Germany, Sweden and the USA. One of her most memorable experiences was judging a class of fifteen Champion bitches in Sweden in 1989 when she was struck by their uniformity both in type and in size. Both Dorothy and her late husband, Stan, have served the Manchu Shih Tzu Society actively for many years, Dorothy going from committee member to Treasurer and then to serve office as Hon. Secretary for thirteen years. Stan was Secretary from 1967 and later became Treasurer.

GREENMOSS: Jeanne and Arnold Leadbitter came into the breed in 1959; they previously had had Terriers and Poodles. The most universally famous dog from this kennel was Ch. Greenmoss Chin-Ki of Meo, whelped in 1961. He won twelve CCs, which included ten Best of Breed, and he was awarded five Utility Group wins at all breeds Championship Shows. The sire of many Champions, not only did he produce three Champions in one of his litters and two in others, but produced one from the first litter he sired and one from the last, when he was twelve and a half years old. Chin-Ki had wonderful presence and was known as 'the Emperor', and was actually sent a kimono from the Far East! He was the sire of Champion offspring in every continent except Africa.

Sixteen Shih Tzu from Greenmoss have gained their UK Championship titles; Chin-Ki and Ch Greenmoss Glory Bee held the top stud dog award for several years. Ch. Fei-Ying of Greenmoss, winner of sixteen CCs, held the breed record in bitches for many years. In fact it was equalled by another bitch from the kennel, Ch. Greenmoss Bee in a Bonnet, who was then retired. Another triumph for Greenmoss was when Int. Ch. Golden Peregrine of Elfann was Reserve Best in Show at Windsor, and at the British Utility Breed Association's Championship Show Ch. Greenmoss Bees-Knees went Reserve Best in Show.

Both Mr and Mrs Leadbitter recall their very first Challenge Certificate win. This was at the Ladies' Kennel Association Show, then held in London. Mei-Saki of Greenmoss was only ten

UK & Italian Ch. Greenmoss Golden Peregrine of Elfann (Sing-Hi of Lhakang – Bobbin of Elfann). Bred by Miss E. M. Evans and owned by A. and J. Leadbitter.

Photo by Kenneth Graham, courtesy Mrs G. Widdrington.

and a half months old and won a Junior Warrant on the same day, later going on to hold the title of Champion. The Leadbitters have judged in many countries abroad and the Greenmoss affix is well represented in Europe, including the Scandinavian countries, Canada, the USA, South America, Brazil, Australia, New Zealand and the Far East. They feel, though, that the breed is not generally as sound as it was, and that some of the lovely heads and oriental expressions are being lost. In some Shih Tzu the eyes are not set wide enough apart, neither are they so lustrous, nor so large as they should be. They are also concerned that some breeders seem to be striving for straight fronts in the Shih Tzu today, and this is something which is simply not possible in a breed which is low to the ground and with a 'barrelled' rib-cage. They also notice some Shih Tzu being too close behind and rather straight in stifle, leading to a lack of typical drive in the hind action.

HARROPINE: Michael and Dee Harper made up their first Champion, Ch. Telota Anouska, in 1979 and their first home-bred Champion, Ch. Harropine China Town, followed in 1983. Since then there have been a further four Champions: Ch. Harropine Christmas Carol, Ch Harropine Lord of The Rings, Ch Harropine Odyssey and Ch Harropine Icarus, now the holder of twenty-two CCs, a record number for a solid colour in the breed. Three other Harropine-bred champions are owned by others in the UK, one of these being Mr and Mrs K. Rawlings' Ch. Harropine Chaka Khan, who won the Utility Group at Crufts in 1987. Both Michael and Dee Harper have awarded Challenge Certificates in the breed since 1987, and they urge present-day breeders to study closely the early Champions of the breed, especially the first, Ch. Ta Chi of Taishan. In doing so, they will be able to decide whether or not they are really breeding to type which they should do in order to retain the unique qualities of this lovely breed.

Harropine Abroad: The Harper's breeding has met with considerable success abroad and the kennel has Champion stock carrying the Harropine affix in South Africa, Denmark, France, Finland and Eire.

Ch. Harropine China Town (Tarralenka Chung Tien of Trisula – Ch. Telota Anouska).

*Ch. Harropine
Christmas Carol
(Snaefell Carry On
Regardless – Tanzu
Mie Ecc-Laire of
Harropine).*

*Ch. Harropine
Icarus (Ch.
Santosha Sunking –
Harropine
Thornbird).*

*Photo by
Carol Ann Johnson.*

Ch. Hashannah Take Me To The Top (Ch. Weatsom Little Big Man of Hashannah – Ch. Weatsom My Fair Lady).
Franks.

Ch. Hashannah Hot Pursuit (Ch. Weatsom Little Big Man of Hashannah – Ch. Weatsom My Fair Lady of Hashannah).
Franks.

HASHANAH: Judy Franks did not become involved with Shih Tzu until 1984, but her dogs have met with considerable success. Her foundation bitch, Ch. Weatsom My Fair Lady, gained her title and went on to produce litter sister and brother Ch. Hashanah Take Me To The Top and Ch. Hashanah Hot Pursuit. The former gained her title in 1991 at only seventeen months old and won a Utility Group and two Reserve Groups, becoming Top Shih Tzu 1991. Her brother, Hot Pursuit, also made up in 1991, was runner-up to his sister and their success makes their dam Top Brood Bitch for 1991. Other Champions not bred by Mrs Franks are Ch. Harropine Timpani of Hashanah and Ch. Weatsom Little Big Man of Hashanah, who has also had a Reserve Group award and is a Champion Stakes winner.

HUXLOR: Mrs Pat Lord has been involved with the breed for fifteen years and has campaigned three Shih Tzu to their Championship titles: Ch. Harropine Super Trooper, Ch. Reubicia Becka of Huxlor and Ch. Huxlor Escudos. In 1989 she imported Louwan Winning Colors At Huxlor from the USA, who has so far gained two CCs. Mrs Lord has judged the breed in Sweden where her choice for Best of Breed went on to gain Best in Show.

*Ch. Gorseycop
Splendid Summer
(Ch. Dominic of
Telota – Gorseycop
Georgette).*
P. Pickburn.

JANMAYEN: Anne Pickburn's parents, Sheila and the late Charles Duke, were committee members of the Shih Tzu Club for many years. Charles was its Hon. Secretary for thirteen years and then became Vice Chairman before his retirement from office. Anne started showing in 1978 and Sheila and Anne now breed in partnership under the Janmayen affix. Their bitch Ch. Janmayen Bianca gained her title in June 1985 and was retired the same year, having been Top Puppy in the breed the year before. Bianca is the dam of Int. Ch. Janmayen Christmas Rose who gained her Championship titles in France, Spain and Italy. Three other Champions campaigned by Anne Pickburn are: Ch. Gorseycop Splendid Summer, bred by Mrs Hoare, who gained her last Reserve CC from the Veteran Class and was a Veteran of the Year finalist in 1985; Ch. Snaefell Katrina of Janmayen, bred by Mrs Dadds; and her most recent Champion, Ch. Snaefell Imperial Rose of Janmayen, owned in partnership with her breeder Mrs Dadds, and who gained her crown with a Best in Show win at the Shih Tzu Club of Wales and Western Counties Show early in 1992. Anne Pickburn and her mother show less regularly now as Anne has a young daughter, and they breed only when they wish to retain a puppy. Anne has commented that she feels the breed has now become rather too popular, with the resultant problems of rescue and untypical specimens being shown as 'show prospects'. She feels that the influx of American and Swedish blood now in the UK needs to be used carefully, but, provided that it is used correctly, it should benefit the breed.

Sheila Duke first awarded CCs in 1977 and one of the highlights of her judging career was awarding the breed record holder, Ch. Firefox of Santosha, his first CC at WELKS (West of England Ladies Kennel Society) in 1986, this from the Graduate class. Shih Tzu were one of three breeds in which Charles awarded CCs and daughter, Anne, first judged at Championship level in 1981, since when she has judged in Sweden and Germany and has other Scandinavian appointments during 1992.

*Ch. Jardhu Waffles
Wu (Ch. Greenmoss
Glory Bee – Wen
Chengsian of
Glengall).*

David J. Lindsay.

*Ch. Wendolyn Wunda
Wizard of Jardhu
(Ch. Santosha
Sunking – Wendolyn
Wilma).*

David J. Lindsay.

Ch. Jardhu Myz-Sunn (Ch. Santosha Royal Flush – Jardhu Mischievous Mi-Zee).
   David J. Lindsay.

JARDHU: Jim and Vicki Grugan have been prominent and successful breeders and exhibitors of Shih Tzu in Scotland and Vicki is currently Hon. Secretary of the Shih Tzu Club of Scotland. Amongst their top winning stock was Ch. Jardhu Waffles Wu, born in April 1979 and who so sadly died on New Year's Day of 1992. Winner of fourteen CCs and six Reserve CCs, he was *Dog World's* Top Winning Shih Tzu in 1983 and won Best of Breed at Crufts in 1985. A Pedigree Chum Veteran Stakes finalist in 1986 and 1990, he was also three times runner-up. He won Best Veteran at the British Utility Breeds Association (BUBA) Show in 1989. A grandson of Waffles Wu, Ch. Wendolyn Wunda Wizard of Jardhu, gained his title in 1990 and has six CCs. One of Waffles Wu's nephews, Ch Jardhu Myz-Sunn, gained his title in 1991.

KARETH: Jim Peat owned his first Shih Tzu, a black and white, in 1970 and though he admits that she was "not the greatest of Shih Tzu" and never really got a full show coat, she was to have a great affect on his future life. When she was mated to Ch. Wyesarge Chinki Tou of Greenmoss in 1972 she produced a litter of two dogs and one bitch. Mr Peat retained the bitch, Kareth Krishna, who won eight CCs with six Reserve CCs and held the title of Top Winning Bitch in 1975 and 1976. She was the first Scottish-bred and owned Champion in the breed. It was sad that she did not breed on for her offspring developed fading puppy syndrome, but she lived to the ripe old age of fifteen years. Yantoreen Sze Moo joined the Kareth kennel and, mated to Whitethroat Chinese Panda, produced a lovely black and white male called Kareth Kestrel. Owned by the late Mrs M. Young, he was campaigned throughout his career by Mr Peat, gaining his crown in 1980 under the full name of Ch. Kareth Kestrel of Ritoung.

   Mr Peat has always followed the policy of producing a small but sturdy dog with good heavy bone and a good head. Santosha Seraphim was given as a present and this sturdy but typically correct bitch was to have a great effect. In her first litter to Gay Widdrington's Lhakang Babu of Bodnic she produced Ch. Kareth Khoir Angel, a bright red, solid gold. It was at Crufts in 1982

Ch. Kareth Khoir Angel (Lhakang Babu of Bodinic – Santosha Seraphim).

Ch. Kareth Kestral of Ritoung (Whitethroat Chinese Panda – Yantoreen Sze Moo).

Pearce.

Ch. & Sw. Ch. Kareth Kummupance (Keltina Sheng Tan Chieh – Santosha Seraphim).

that she gained her title, making her the first solid gold Shih Tzu Champion, and she was Top Bitch for 1982. Mated to Keltina Sheng Tan Chieh, Khoir Angel produced the black and white dog, Ch. Kareth Kumuppance who later moved to Sweden where he also gained his Swedish title.

Kareth Khamelion, owned by Mr and Mrs Hickey in Dublin, was mated to Ch. Firefox of Santosha, and produced a litter which included Irish Ch. Koleus of Lyre. His litter sister, Ch. Kareth Kismet of Lyre, was made up in 1987 and won twenty-six first prizes at Championship shows before ever winning a second and, indeed, was never placed lower than third. She won fifteen CCs and was the breed's first Irish-bred UK Champion. She was Top Shih Tzu Bitch in Britain in 1987 and 1988. Another great achievement from this kennel was that Ch. Kareth Kharisma, born in 1987, was made up at the age of only thirteen months.

Jim Peat first awarded CCs in Shih Tzu at the Scottish Kennel Club in 1979. Highlights of his judging career include judging the Manchu Shih Tzu Society's Championship Show in 1982, the Shih Tzu Club of Finland in 1985, the Shih Tzu Club of Sweden in 1987 and on two occasions he has judged at the Shih Tzu International Club in Germany. He looks forward to judging the breed at Crufts in 1993. Mr Peat feels that breeders must be careful to maintain the true Shih Tzu in both type and temperament. He points out that the Shih Tzu action can only be seen when dogs are moved at the correct speed and, being a short-legged breed, they are not meant to be raced around the ring at high speeds.

Kareth abroad: GB & Swed. Ch. Kareth Kumuppance is now in Sweden where he is making his mark and Kareth Curtain Call, who produced young CC winning offspring in her first litter, is with Major Hasle in Sweden. In Finland, Finnish Ch. Kareth Khan, a son of Kharisma, flies the flag of the Kareth kennel.

*Ch. Kuire Secret
Simon (Camglia
Fuzzacker – Ch.
Charka of Kuire).*

KEYTOR: Susan and Ellen Johnson have been involved with the breed for over thirty years, Mrs Johnson actually went out to buy a Pekingese and came home with two Shih Tzu! The first Shih Tzu shown by Susan had won two CCs by the age of ten months and went on to become Ch. Keytor Sweet Charity. Over the years they have owned nine UK Champions, all but one having been bred at Keytor. Sadly, in 1991, at the age of only five years, they lost Ch. Keytor Sebastian. He was made up in three straight shows, and was a multiple CC winner who had won the Utility Group at Windsor and Reserve in the Group at Crufts.
Keytor Abroad: Much Keytor-bred stock has gone abroad to Europe, Canada, the USA, Australia and to Argentina where, in the late 1970s, one of the Johnsons' exports went Top Bitch all breeds. They sent Aust. Ch. Keytor Christopher Robin to Australia, and he was to make a big impact on the breed. He was Top Dog for two years and played an important part in bringing down the size of the breed as it was then in Australia.

KUIRE: Mrs Josephine Johnson's earliest connection with the breed was in 1954, and she has awarded Challenge Certificates in Shih Tzu since 1977. She has judged in Germany, Norway and Sweden and had the honour of officiating at Crufts in 1987. In 1989 she judged a record entry at the Scottish Shih Tzu Club's Championship Show. In 1971 Mrs Johnson bred the dog who was to become the breed record holder until 1988. This was Ch. Kuire Hermes of Antartica, owned by Mr and Mrs K. B. Rawlings. Her own Ch. Charka of Kuire gained her title in 1983 but was sadly injured after winning her third and crowning CC and did not manage to get back in the ring. She was the Top Shih Tzu Bitch in 1983, and in 1984 Mrs Johnson's Ch. Kuire Secret Simon, who amassed ten CCs and seven Reserves, was the Top Shih Tzu male. In Norway Kuire Troubador gained his Norwegian Championship title.

LANSU and ELFANN: Mrs Sylvia Rawlings, formerly Mrs Hoyle, firstly owned the Lansu affix and then that of Elfann, owned jointly with Jenny Taylor, daughter of Miss E. M. Evans. The Lansu prefix was originally owned by her late husband, Ian Hoyle. When the Hoyles decided to venture into breeding they decided to breed for the Elfann 'type' and to continue Miss Evans' gold line. Mrs Rawlings' earliest connection with this breed was in 1966. Ch. Lansu Fragrant Cloud, owned and bred by Mrs Rawlings, gained her title in 1978. Her other Champions include: Ch. Golden Heidi of Elfann, Ch. Golden Summertime of Elfann, both of whom have been Veteran Stakes winners, and Ch. Elfann Golden Posy of Lansu, who won Best of Breed at Crufts at the age of two. Up to Mr Hoyle's death in 1979 the Lansu kennel only bred ten litters and Mrs Rawlings feels lucky to have achieved so much in just a few years of breeding. There have been two Elfann litters since going into partnership with Jenny Taylor: Int. Ch. Elfann Cloth of Gold from the first litter lives in Switzerland, and a dog and bitch from the second litter have been exported to Sweden.

Mrs Rawlings considers her first ever judging appointment to be one of the highlights of her career. At this, a breed club show in Sweden, two of her young winners, both grand-daughters of Int. Ch. Kurts Boy of Lansu, went on to become International Champions and Best in Show winners at International shows. She awarded CCs in the UK for the first time at W.E.L.K.S. in 1987 and has since judged a breed club Championship Show here and had a record entry at B.U.B.A. in 1991. Other judging appointments have been in Finland, Ireland and Germany. Sylvia Rawlings feels that breed type as it was even ten years ago seems to be disappearing. In her opinion, the breed is losing the beautiful heads and expressions, with correct nose and eye placement. The typical Shih Tzu movement which reaches in front and drives from behind, really covering the ground is, she thinks, becoming hard to find, as is the 'barrel' rib cage. She also comments that narrow fronts and rears seem to be in the majority.

Lansu abroad: In the Scandinavian countries there have been many top winners carrying Mrs Rawlings' breeding, with kennels in Norway, Sweden and Finland all importing stock from Lansu between 1974 and 1976. Int. Ch. Kurt's Boy of Lansu was the first English bred, Swedish owned International Champion and has had a great influence on the breed. At his very first show at the age of eight months he went Best of Breed under the late Reg Gadsden. Int. Ch. Lansu Heidi's Fair Lady did remarkably well at her first show in Sweden at the age of eighteen months, and gained her international title scarcely one year later. Litter sisters to Fair Lady are Irish Ch. Lansu Treasure from Heidi and Finnish Ch. Lansu to Heidi, all three of whom were hand-reared from the age of five days. Finnish Ch. Annabelle of Lansu, Swedish Ch. Lansu Joyous Spirit and Int. Ch. My Choice From Lansu are others carrying titles abroad. There are also three American Lansu Champions and one with an Australian and New Zealand title. Lansu Easter Time of Elanzo, from the Hoyles' very first litter, produced Elanzo Gold Digger who went on to sire numerous champions worldwide.

LHAKANG: Registered as a kennel name in 1946 (meaning 'Temple of the Gods'), Mrs Gay Widdrington's Lhakang kennel was originally founded just after the outbreak of World War II and is now the oldest Shih Tzu kennel in existence in the UK. Mrs Widdrington bought a black and white bitch puppy, Mee Na, from Lady Brownrigg, this being ostensibly as a pet to keep her company, as her husband had been called up for service. The bitch was of the second generation from the first three imported to Britain from China in 1930, and Lady Brownrigg only parted

Mrs Gay Widdrington with two young puppies from her Lhakang kennel.

with her on the condition that Mrs Widdrington helped her to establish the breed which was then very rare. Mee Na led to a life-long interest in the breed. Mrs Widdrington still has vivid recollections of the early dogs and she has done her best to preserve their essential characteristics. Mee Na had one litter during the war, but this was to her sire as he was the only male available.

Following the war, in 1946, Mrs Widdrington helped to rebuild the Shih Tzu Club, tracing former members and rekindling enthusiasm among the war-weary. Breeding stock had been at a low ebb but new import lines soon arrived to swell the gene pool and the Lhakang kennel carried out careful, selective breeding over many years. It helped not only to introduce but also to stabilise new lines from China and elsewhere, thereby establishing the breed on a broader basis. It is thanks to the efforts of Mrs Widdrington that the breed in Britain has remained in such a healthy state. In the late 1940s Mrs Widdrington and her mother decided to establish a true-breeding rich golden strain through the bitch line of Ishuh Tzu, who had been imported from Shanghai, and it is this colour which still flourishes in the kennel. The line has also spread to many countries abroad.

In 1952, Ch. Mao-Mao of Lhakang, a daughter of Mee Na, produced an outstanding black and white litter to Ch. Yu Mo of Boydon. Four of the litter were to become Champions and it was this litter which really established the Lhakang kennel, founding an important and continuing line. By the early 1960s this was the top-winning Shih Tzu kennel in Britain and to date has produced thirteen Champions. Mrs Widdrington's interest lies more in breeding and rearing than in exhibiting; her aim has always been to produce reliable breeding stock. In 1964, after her black and white Ch. Soong of Lhakang gained her title, she retired from active showing but has helped to establish many other kennels over the years. A son of Soong, Sing-hi of Lhakang produced two famous sons in Int. Ch. Greenmoss Golden Peregrin of Elfann and Ch. Jen-ki-ko, both of whom had an important impact on the breed.

From her current stock, Mrs Widdrington values highly her red-gold Lhakang Cherubim, who is the dam of UK and Finnish Ch. Lhakang Cassius and of Nord. Ch. Lhakang Celandine. Lhakang Babu of Bodinic, a solid red-gold, started a strong new line, for he was sire of Cherubim and also Susan and David Crossley's Ch. Santosha Sunking and Jim Peat's Ch. Kareth Khoir Angel. In 1989 Lhakang produced a rather special litter of five puppies. Amanda of Lhakang, a daughter of Sunking, was the dam and the sire was Nordic and Swedish Ch. Boreas Golden Overlord, whose frozen semen was sent over by Fru Reiden Pettersen in Norway for artificial insemination. Although the reason for using AI was to counteract a build-up of an hereditary problem, the English Kennel Club has so far refused to register the litter.

It was in 1951 that Gay Widdrington became a specialist judge of Shih Tzu and has judged at Championship Shows regularly ever since. She has enjoyed seeing the progress of the breed worldwide on her many judging appointments during the 70s and 80s. She and her husband, Francis, live in the ancestral home in the wilds of Northumberland and the dogs live as family pets, with the run of the parks and woodland. Because her own dogs are never confined she always prefers to place her puppies in homes where they are able to live as family members rather than as kennel dogs. In 1971 Mrs Widdrington produced her informative little Shih Tzu Handbook which was illustrated by her daughter and has been a great help to breeders and enthusiasts past and present.

Now breeding on a small scale, and with a continued interest in the breed worldwide, Mrs Widdrington has retired from judging and from committee work, but she held a whole string of offices in former years. These included Treasurer and Chairman of the Shih Tzu Club, Founder, Chairman and President of the Manchu Shih Tzu Society, Patron of the Shih Tzu Club of New South Wales (Australia) and of the Shih Tzu Club of Scotland. She is an Honorary Life Member of the American Shih Tzu Club and the Shih Tzu Club of Finland. She writes many valuable articles and breed columns for publication throughout the world, including the UK canine press and breed club newsletters.

LHAKANG ABROAD

USA: A black and white dog, Ching-yea of Lhakang, went out to the USA in 1966. This, however, was several years before before the Shih Tzu was officially recognised by the American Kennel Club, preventing him, of course, from gaining his title. But that did not stop him from being listed as an 'All-time Top Producer', gaining his Registry of Merit award (ROM) for having sired eleven American Champions.

Finland: Ch. Lhakang Cassius, sire of twelve Champions, is now owned by Eija Verlander in Finland. He is sire of the 1991 World Winner, Dortmund – Ch. Jem-Gem Choir Angel, owned by Ritva Nissila, also of Finland. Ch. Lhakang Casper, owned by Ansa and Olli Pennanen, is also producing top-winning stock and is a younger sibling to Cassius. Both Cassius and Casper are by Tor Ra Lon, who is similar in type to Sing-hi. Swedish and Finnish Ch. Araminta, also in Finland, is a grand-daughter of Mrs Widdrington's much-loved Cherubim.

Norway: Black and white Nord. Ch. Lhakang Jolyon was the foundation stud of the Boreas kennel of Major Borre Hasle in Norway. Jolyon is now the sire of fifteen Champions and is grand-sire of at least thirty-five more. Two grandchildren of Jolyon were sent back to England in 1987, a dog, Boreas Chinese Spirit, going to the Santosha kennel and Boreas Chinese Starlet, a bitch, to Lhakang. They have produced some fine offspring and have helped to strengthen the

Ch. Rosaril The Chimney Sweep (Ch. Santosha Sunking – Ch. Rosaril Modesty Blaize).
E. Stephenson.

black and white lines. Nord. Ch. Lhakang Celandine was the Top Shih Tzu in Norway in 1986 and 1987. Owned by Major Hasle, she is the dam of eight Champions. Celandine was also sired by Tor Ra Lon. Other descendants of Cherubim in Norway are Ch. Lhakang Bells A Ringing and Nordic and Swedish Ch. Lhakang Anneli who was Top Bitch in Norway in 1990.
Australia: Australian Ch. Lhakang Chen Pu-Yi, a litter-brother of Cherubim, has twelve Champion descendants.

ROSARIL: Mrs Eunice Stephenson's first two Champions were Ch. Jaivonne Glimmer of Hope, made up in 1980, and Ch. Rosaril Modesty Blaize. She then bred Ch. Rosaril The Chimney Sweep, one of only three black representatives of the breed to gain their titles and, of those, one was actually registered as black but paled with maturity. Chimney Sweep gained his first two CCs while still a Junior and gained his title at the beginning of 1988. In 1990 Mrs Stephenson made up a fourth Champion, Ch. Rosaril Delilah. Her Championship show judging appointments have included three breed club shows and one general Championship Show. Mrs Stephenson is worried that the whole concept of the Shih Tzu is in danger of changing; she is concerned about the breed becoming too light in frame and small in rib-cage. She also considers that swan necks and a gradual increase in length of leg are points of construction which need to be carefully watched. It is a substantial cause of concern to Mrs Stephenson that some breeders seem to be aiming primarily for glamour.

SANTOSHA: Susan and David Crossley have had a great deal of success in the breed and are owners of the famous Ch. Firefox of Santosha, bred by Messrs Easdon and Martin, who is the breed record holder with thirty-five CCs. His greatest successes include one Reserve Best in Show award, two Group wins and two Reserve Group wins at all breeds Championship Shows.

Santosha Sunking (Lhakang Babu of Bodinic – Santosha Sunset).

Ch. Santosha Tiger Lily (Keytor Chatterbox – Santosha Sunbeam).

Jean Luc.

Firefox was Top Sire in 1991, and over the last five years a dog from the Crossley kennels – Ch. Firefox of Santosha, Ch. Santosha Sunking and Ch. Santosha Royal Flush – has held this title. Ch. Santosha Rambling Rose, made up at the age of three, was the first Shih Tzu Champion from this kennel, and she was one of four Champions gaining Best of Breed at Crufts. The other Champions which have come from the Santosha kennel are Ch. Santosha Bewitched, Ch. Santosha Sundown, Ch. Santosha Bewitching of Janmayen and Ch. Santosha Tiger Lily.

Santosha breeding has been exported to Australia, USA, Norway, Sweden, South Africa, Denmark and Germany and some of these have gained titles abroad. Susan and David have also judged in many countries abroad and had the honour of judging the breed at the World Show in Dortmund, Germany, in 1991. Susan judged bitches and David officiated for dogs, and for their Best of Breed they jointly selected Swedish and Finnish Ch. Jem-Gem Choir Angel, who I was pleased to see pulled out in the Group.

SNAEFELL: In 1955 Audrey Dadds, like so many other top breeders, began by buying a pet Shih Tzu and subsequently fell for the breed, finding both showing and breeding an absorbing hobby. She has never bred extensively but usually in order to keep a line going or for a show puppy. The majority of other puppies in a litter have almost always gone to pet homes where they could remain as much loved pets for the rest of their lives. Mrs Dadds has been a somewhat reluctant exporter but she has allowed a few of her dogs to go to friends abroad.

She has bred eight UK Champions, six of which she has owned personally. Ch. Snaefells Limited Edition is one of her most recent success stories; in 1991 he won the progeny class at the Manchu breed club Championship Show and the progeny all breed stakes class at Windsor Championship Show, while still under three years of age. His breeding is interesting for he has an American Champion sire from old American lines, and he is the first Shih Tzu with any American parentage to gain his title in the UK. Line-bred to Ch. Newroots Nankipoo of Snaefell, he is by Am. Ch. Din Ho Rupert T. Bear and out of her own Snaefells Irma La Douce. Among the other Champions from this kennel are Ch. Buttons of Snaefells and Ch. Newroots Nankipoo of Snaefell, who amassed thirteen CCs and was Reserve in the Utility Group at Bournemouth in 1972.

Mrs Dadds feels that her best dog has been Ch. Newroots Nankipoo of Snaefell and her best bitch, Ch. Snaefells Imperial Imp, with Ch. Snaefells Limited Edition close on their heels. Looking back, Mrs Dadds considers that the first Champion in the breed, Ch. Ta Chi Of Taishan, is the type to aim for as she had the overall balance which is lacking in many specimens of the breed today. Mrs Dadds makes the following comments on the breed which, rather than run the risk of changing them by my own interpretation, I include here in their entirety:

"We have too many different types, many too low on the leg, and with the American influence too much height of leg needs watching, also bad toplines which get covered up by tail furnishings.

"Naturally, there is need of improvement in coat and presentation since 1949 (when Ta Chi became a Champion) but too much emphasis on coat will be to the detriment of the breed. This already shows by so many having lost the lovely smooth, flowing arrogant action, which should be typical of the breed. There should be no reason why breeders can't have the best of both worlds: a correct body and a glorious coat.

"With the many imports in recent years, it is most important that breeders make full use of the good that is in and behind these animals, for they have much to give which can help to improve our own. They must equally be careful to discard the points which we, in this country, do not want. This way we should go from strength to strength, whilst retaining the Shih Tzu as we have always known and loved it."

Mrs Dadds first awarded CCs in the breed in 1966 and she last gave CCs at the Shih Tzu Club's Championship Show in 1990. She has decided not to take on any further appointments.

Snaefell abroad: Despite being a "reluctant exporter", Mrs Dadds' Snaefell breeding has met with much success abroad with Snaefell-bred Champions in Australia, South Africa and Sweden, and Int. Spanish and Portuguese Ch. Snaefells Little Flower has been a Group winner. In the 1980s Australian Ch. Snaefells Anastasia, owned by Mrs Thelma Burnell, won Best Exhibit in Group 7 at Kilmore Championship Show, and as early as the 1950s Australian Ch. Hia Nan of Snaefell (litter sister to Ch. Snaefell Sindi Lu of Antartica), owned by Gwen Teele, was exported by Mr Rawlings.

*Ch. Newroots
Nankipoo of Snaefell
(Ch. Greenmoss Chin-
Ki of Meo – Ho Yan of
Newroots).*

Anne Roslyn Williams.

*Ch. Snaefells Imperial
Imp (Ch. Newroots
Nankipoo of Snaefell
– Snaefell Queen of
the Snow).*

Frank Garwood.

*Ch. Snaefells Limited
Edition (Am. Ch. Din
Ho Rupert T. Bear –
Snaefell Irma La
Douce).*

Russell Fine Art.

TAONAN Diana Harding, who was Hon. Secretary of the Manchu Shih Tzu Club in the 1970s and has been Hon. Secretary of the Shih Tzu Club of South Wales and Western Counties since 1983, first became involved with the breed in 1967. She has awarded Challenge Certificates in Shih Tzu since 1977, and has judged also in Sweden and in Eire. Mrs Harding had the honour of judging the breed for the Centenary of Crufts in 1991 when she had a world record entry of 252. Her Ch. Saranana Chiu Mei of Taonan gained her title in 1973, her first CC having been awarded only four months following whelping a litter of puppies and when, quite incredibly, she was in full coat. Irish Ch. Taonan Tasmin of Lyre was the first Shih Tzu bitch ever to gain her title in Southern Ireland and Irish Ch. Taonan Boris, who gained his title in 1975, had an important influence on the breed in Ireland.

Mrs Harding feels that the movement of the Shih Tzu is vital and is somewhat concerned that rear movement at present is getting rather close. Fronts, she believes, have always been a problem in some lines, and she worries that too much emphasis is put on keeping a good coat and not enough on exercise. She walks her own show dogs and 'oldies' two to three miles on road surface each day. Mrs Harding says that although her dogs have always had good mouths, she feels that the Shih Tzu should not be judged on its mouth, so long as it has a good width of jaw and a strong chin. She feels that a Shih Tzu can a have a wide mouth with only four incisors, and even with six the mouth can be narrow. She also points out that a puppy with six incisors in its first mouth can develop only four when its second teeth come through.

TELOTA: Owing to ill health, Mrs Olive Newson has been compelled to retire from active breeding but much influential stock has come through the Telota kennel over the years. This includes Choo Choo and Ten Sing of Cathay, the former being the grandsire of the famous Ch. Greenmoss Chin-Ki of Meo. Domese of Telota produced two English Champions, Ch. Dominic of Telota and Ch. Don Juan of Telota, as well as two Irish champions. Canadian Ch. Choo Lang of Telota was the leading Canadian Champion of 1972.

WEATSOM: Margaret Stangeland was Top Breeder of Shih Tzu in 1988, 1989, 1990 and 1991. She did not own the breed until 1982, but since then she has bred five Champions: Ch. Weatsom Only You, Ch. Weatsom Tom Thumb and Ch. Weatsom Madam Butterfly, all owner-bred, and Ch. Weatsom My Fair Lady of Hashanah and Ch. Weatsom Little Big Man of Hashanah, owned by Judy Franks.

Readers will appreciate that there have, of course, been many other very successful breeders and exhibitors and, indeed, dogs, but unfortunately it would require a veritable tome to pay full tribute to them all. Ch. Ellingham Kala Nag, bred by Lady Haggerston and owned by Mrs J. Lovely, was a great ambassador for the breed in the 1960s, he won Best of Breed at Crufts in 1963 and 1964, in which year he also took the Utility Group at Manchester. Mr and Mrs E. Carter bred a litter which produced three Shih Tzu Champions and Mr David Iley's Ch. Senousi Be-Pop De Lux broke the bitch CC record, formerly held by Mr and Mrs Leadbitter's Ch. Fei-Ying of Greenmoss. Glenys Dolphin, Thelma Morgan's daughter, has also been much involved with Shih Tzu throughout her life and recently campaigned to her title the gold and white Swedish import, Ch. Anibes Puttin' on the Ritz, bred by Anita Berggren in 1985. She is owned in partnership. Mrs Francis Hickey's Lyre breeding has played a most important part in the Shih

Ch. Anibes Puttin' on the Ritz (Swed. Ch. Whitethroat Jarvis – Nord. Int. Ch. Yringhs No Stuffed Toi for Anibes). *Photo by Carol Ann Johnson.*

Tzu's development in Ireland. Other highly respected Shih Tzu which have not yet been mentioned but which were amongst those selected by well respected Championship judges in a Kennel Club survey carried out in 1989 are Ch. Ya Tung of Antartica, Ch. Fleeting Yu Sing of Antartica and Ch. Ragoosa Golden Raffles.

Chapter Five

THE BREED STANDARD

Before reading the Kennel Club's Breed Standard it is important to understand that any Standard is, in effect, a blue-print of the breed, painted in words rather than pictures. What makes dog showing interesting is that everyone who reads the written word is likely to interpret it in a slightly different way, and so it is that different judges put up different dogs. However, we must all aim to breed and judge to the Standard which has, after all, been compiled by highly knowledgeable people, connected closely with the breed. It is all too easy to read a Standard and to try to make the words fit your own dogs, laying emphasis on the parts of the Standard which fit and conveniently glossing over those which don't. However experienced we may be, it does us all good to re-read the Standard from time to time, if only to consolidate our knowledge and to look at it once again with fresh eyes which may, in turn, lead us to a freshness of perception. The Breed Standard used by the Federation Cynologique International (FCI), approved by the General Assembly on June 23rd and 24th, 1987 in Jerusalem, is exactly as the British Breed Standard. The country of origin of the breed is specified as Tibet and the country of patronage, Great Britain. In America the American Kennel Club has drawn up its own Breed Standard, and this has also been reproduced so that the differences between them can be noted.

THE BRITISH BREED STANDARD

GENERAL APPEARANCE Sturdy, abundantly coated dog with distinctly arrogant carriage and chrysanthemum-like face.
CHARACTERISTICS Intelligent, active and alert.
TEMPERAMENT Friendly and independent.
HEAD & SKULL Head broad, round, wide between eyes. Shock-headed with hair falling well over eyes. Good beard and whiskers, hair growing upwards on the nose giving a

distinctly chrysanthemum-like effect. Muzzle of ample width, square, short, not wrinkled, flat and hairy. Nose black but dark liver in liver or liver marked dogs and about one inch from tip to definite stop. Nose level or slightly tip-tilted. Top of nose leather should be on a line with or slightly below lower eyerim. Wide open nostrils. Downpointed nose highly undesirable, as are pinched nostrils. Pigmentation on muzzle as unbroken as possible.

EYES Large, dark, round, placed well apart but not prominent. Warm expression. In liver or liver marked dogs, lighter eye colour permissible. No white of eye showing.

EARS Large, with long leathers, carried drooping. Set slightly below crown of skull, so heavily coated they appear to blend into hair of neck.

MOUTH Wide, slightly undershot or level. Lips level.

NECK Well proportioned, nicely arched. Sufficient length to carry head proudly.

FOREQUARTERS Shoulders well laid back. Legs short, and muscular with ample bone, as straight as possible, consistent with broad chest being well let down.

BODY Longer between withers and root of tail than height of withers, well coupled and sturdy, chest broad and deep, shoulders firm, back level.

HINDQUARTERS Legs short and muscular with ample bone. Straight when viewed from the rear. Thighs well rounded and muscular. Legs looking massive on account of wealth of hair.

FEET Rounded, firm and well padded, appearing big on account of wealth of hair.

TAIL Heavily plumed carried gaily well over back. Set on high. Height approximately level with that of skull to give a balanced outline.

GAIT/MOVEMENT Arrogant, smooth-flowing, front legs reaching well forward, strong rear action and showing full pad.

COAT Long, dense, not curly, with good undercoat. Slight wave permitted. Strongly recommended that hair on head tied up.

COLOUR All colours permissible, white blaze on forehead and white tip to tail highly desirable in parti-colours.

WEIGHT & SIZE 4.5 to 8.1 kg. (10-18 lb.). Ideal weight 4.5-7.3 kg. (10-16 lb.). Height at withers not more than 26.7 cm (10 1/2 in.), type and breed characteristics of the utmost importance and on no account to be sacrificed to size alone.

FAULTS Any departure from the foregoing points should be considered a fault and the seriousness with which the fault should be regarded should be in exact proportion to its degree.

NOTE Male animals should have two apparently normal testicles fully descended into the scrotum.

Reproduced by kind permission of the English Kennel Club.

THE AMERICAN BREED STANDARD
(Revised 1988)

GENERAL APPEARANCE

The Shih Tzu is a sturdy, lively and alert toy dog with long flowing double coat. Befitting his noble Chinese ancestry as a highly valued, prized companion and palace pet, the Shih Tzu is proud of bearing, has a distinctly arrogant carriage with head well up and tail curved over the back. Although there has always been a considerable size variation, the

Shih Tzu must be compact, solid, carrying good weight and substance. Even though a toy dog, the Shih Tzu must be subject to the same requirements of soundness and structure prescribed for all breeds, and any deviation from the ideal described in the Standard should be penalized to the extent of the deviation. Structural faults common to all breeds are as undesirable in the Shih Tzu as in any other breed, regardless of whether or not such faults are specifically mentioned in the Standard.

SIZE, PROPORTION, SUBSTANCE

Size – Ideally, height at withers is 9 to 10 1/2 inches; but not less than 8 inches nor more than 11 inches. Ideally, weight of mature dogs – 9 to 16 pounds.

Proportion – Length between withers and root of tail is slightly longer than height at withers. The Shih Tzu must never be so high stationed as to appear leggy, nor so low stationed as to appear dumpy or squatty.

Substance – Regardless of size, the Shih Tzu is always compact, solid and carries good weight and substance.

HEAD

Head – Round, broad, wide between eyes, its size in balance with the overall size of dog being neither too large nor too small.

Fault: Narrow head, close-set eyes.

Expression – Warm, sweet, wide-eyed, friendly and trusting. An overall well-balanced and pleasant expression supercedes the importance of individual parts. Care should be taken to look and examine well beyond the hair to determine if what is seen is the actual head and expression rather than an image created by grooming technique.

Eyes – Large, round, not prominent, placed well apart, looking straight ahead. Very dark. Lighter on liver pigmented dogs and blue pigmented dogs.

Fault: Small close-set or light eyes; excessive eye white.

Ears – Large, set slightly below crown of skull; heavily coated.

Skull – Domed.

Stop – There is a definite stop.

Muzzle – Square, short, unwrinkled, with good cushioning, set no lower than bottom eye rim; never downturned. Ideally, no longer than 1 inch from tip of nose to stop, although length may vary slightly in relation to overall size of dog. Front of muzzle should be flat; lower lip and chin not protruding and definitely never receding.

Fault: Snipiness, lack of definite stop.

Nose – Nostrils are broad, wide and open.

Pigmentation – Nose, lips, eyerims are black on all colors, except liver on liver pigmented dogs and blue on blue pigmented dogs.

Fault: Pink on nose, lips or eye rims.

Bite – Undershot. Jaw is broad and wide. A missing tooth or slightly misaligned teeth should not be too severely penalized. Teeth and tongue should not show when mouth is closed.

Fault: Overshot bite.

NECK, TOPLINE, BODY

Of utmost importance is an overall well-balanced dog with no exaggerated features.

Neck – Well set-on flowing smoothly into shoulders; of sufficient length to permit natural high head carriage and in balance with height and length of dog.

Topline – Level.

Body – Short-coupled and sturdy with no waist or tuck-up. The Shih Tzu is slightly longer than tall.

Fault: Legginess.

Chest – Broad and deep with good spring-of-rib, however, not barrel-chested. Depth of ribcage should extend to just below elbow. Distance from elbow to withers is a little greater than from elbow to ground.

Croup – Flat.

Tail – Set on high, heavily plumed, carried in curve well over back. Too loose, too tight, too flat, or too low set a tail is undesirable and should be penalized to extent of deviation.

FOREQUARTERS

Shoulders – Well-angulated, well laid-back, well laid-in, fitting smoothly into body.

Legs – Straight, well-boned, muscular, set well-apart and under chest, with elbows set close to body.

Pasterns – Strong, perpendicular.

Dewclaws – May be removed.

Feet – Firm, well-padded, point straight ahead.

HINDQUARTERS

Angulation of hindquarters should be in balance with forequarters.

Legs – Well-boned, muscular, and straight when viewed from rear with well-bent stifles, not close set but in line with forequarters.

Hocks – Well let down, perpendicular.

Fault: Hyperextension of hocks.

Dewclaws – May be removed.

Feet – Firm, well-padded, point straight ahead.

COAT

Coat – Luxurious, double-coated, dense, long, and flowing. Slight wave permissible. Hair on top of head is tied up.

Fault: Sparse coat, single coat, curly coat.

Trimming – Feet, bottom of coat, and anus may be done for neatness and to facilitate movement.

Fault: Excessive trimming.

COLOR AND MARKINGS

All are permissible and to be considered equally.

GAIT

The Shih Tzu moves straight and must be shown at its own natural speed, neither raced nor strung-up, to evaluate its smooth, flowing, effortless movement with good front reach and equally strong rear drive, level topline, naturally high head carriage, and tail carried in gentle curve over back.

TEMPERAMENT

As the sole purpose of the Shih Tzu is that of a companion and house pet, it is essential that its temperament be out-going, happy, affectionate, friendly and trusting towards all.

Reproduced by kind permission of the American Kennel Club.

Judges sometimes find it difficult to see the expression in a black Sih Tzu, but this is a lovely example. She is Dusky Rose of Bellakerne, still quite a youngster.

Photo by Carol Ann Johnson.

ANALYSIS

HEAD AND EXPRESSSION

The skull shape of the Shih Tzu is one of the characteristic features of the breed and the correct skull for the breed is quite different from that of the Lhasa Apso or the Pekingese. The Shih Tzu skull falls somewhere in the middle, in all respects. The head is broader than that of the Apso and not so flat as that of the Pekingese. In keeping with the shape of the skull, the eyes of the Shih Tzu are round but not so prominent as those of the Pekingese and yet more prominent than those of the Apso; there is also greater width between the eyes than with the Apso. Ideally, there should be no white showing around the eye, though the American Standard penalises only *excessive* eye white. We certainly do not require too large an eye, which is out of proportion with the size of the head. Looking at the Shih Tzu head-on, we can see that the nose is roughly in line with the lower eye-rim, though it may be tilted just slightly upward. A nose which is tilted downwards gives a totally untypical expression.

Looking at the head in profile, the steep stop is clearly evident and, again, we can see the correct angle of the nose, the length from tip to stop being roughly as 1 is to 4 (or 5) from stop to occiput. The length of nose must always be in proportion to the size of the head, and the head should be in balance with the body. There should always be some width to the nostrils for we do not wish to encourage the problem of tight nostrils in the breed. Chin is desirable, but not too much of it. Strength, depth and breadth of chin is usually (but not always) dependent upon the placement of the jaw and teeth. A Shih Tzu with a scissor bite is more likely to lack chin than a dog with a correct, slightly undershot, bite. In reverse, a dog with an uptilted nose runs the risk of appearing a little too strong in underjaw; this also frequently applies to a dog which is rather

Pekingese.

Shih Tzu.

Lhasa Apso.

too undershot. An overshot mouth is a serious fault for it is totally untypical of the breed and destroys the delightful, oriental expression. When the mouth is closed the teeth should not show and the upper lips should close over the lower.

Although the Breed Standard does not mention number of teeth, in an ideal mouth there should be six incisors in both the upper and lower jaw. In order to achieve the width of jaw which is desirable they should be fairly evenly placed. In cases of fewer than five teeth, especially when there are only four or even fewer, there is a high probability that the jaw will not be sufficiently wide. On the other hand, if there are six jumbled, or even six exceptionally small, incisors, there

Profiles

Correct.

Too long, lacking stop.

*Too short
and Peke-
like.*

is a severe risk of the jaw being insufficiently wide. The bite should be slightly undershot or level. Clearly, an overshot bite gives an undesirable expression as can a scissor bite for in both cases it is likely that there will be insufficient underjaw. An excessively undershot jaw also detracts from the expression, albeit in a different way, and such a bite often does not permit the lips to close level with each other. As in any breed, a wry mouth is something to be avoided. In effect we are looking for a fairly square muzzle.

A clear distinction between dogs and bitches should also be evident in the head; the head of the male being somewhat larger and more masculine that that of the bitch which should have a distinctly feminine expression. The ears should be set on below the crown, not so high as on the Pekingese. The American Standard includes the comment that care should be taken to look well beyond the hair, and I feel this is highly relevant for clever hair-dressing can hide a multitude of sins!

Various bites

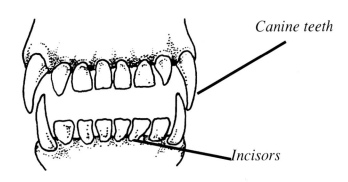

Canine teeth

Correct dentition.

Incisors

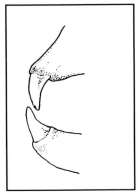

Slightly undershot

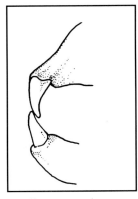

Reverse scissor.

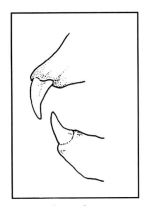

Overshot.

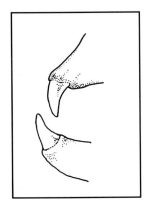

Undershot..

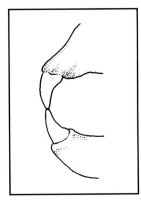

Level.

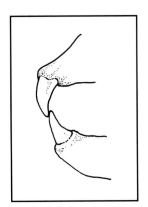

Scissor.

THE NECK AND FOREQUARTERS

Neck and forequarters must of necessity be assessed together, for one has a great bearing on the other. A Shih Tzu which is too upright in shoulder frequently appears short in neck because, as a consequence of the poor shoulder placement, the withers are further forward, giving a somewhat 'stuffy' appearance. This, of course, also affects the movement, but we shall come to that in a moment. The well proportioned neck should be sufficiently well arched and, though it should be of sufficient length to carry the head proudly, it should not be overlong, thereby destroying the balance of the dog. Coat can, as has been said with regard to head-furnishings, hide certain faults, but a good judge can all too easily discover faults in forehand construction, not only when assessing a dog on the table but also on the move. In the Shih Tzu, which is rather low to the ground, it would be impossible to have absolutely straight front legs (as, for example, those of a Terrier) for they would simply not accommodate the depth and breadth of chest which is required for the breed. The British and FCI Standard asks that the legs be "as straight as possible", carefully allowing just a little latitude, while the American Standard requires them to be "straight", something that is not easy to achieve, given the shape of the Shih Tzu's ribcage. Certainly the legs should be straight enough so that the feet are able to point forward, turning neither in nor out. The legs should be muscular and neither too heavy nor too fine in bone; the British and FCI Standards use the word "ample", the American Standard, however, calls for the Shih Tzu's legs to be "well-boned".

BODY AND BALANCE

The withers are to be found at the uppermost point of the scapuli and the Standard requires the Shih Tzu to be longer between withers and root of tail than the height from ground to withers. It does not, however, say how much longer but when one takes into account the fact that the Standard also requires a sturdy and well coupled dog, with a broad, deep chest and a level back it becomes clear that one should not be looking for extreme length. Looking at a well balanced Shih Tzu in profile, we should be able to imagine a line running perpendicularly to the ground from the rearmost point of the scapula, through the back of the elbow. The humerus should not be too short or the dog will lack facility of forehand extension which, depending upon the correctness of the hind construction, can cause all sorts of problems in the movement of the dog.

Another problem which can be caused by the combination of too short an upper arm and a correct shoulder is that the dog is lower at the front that the back, once again destroying the overall balance, not to mention the topline! The chest should be broad and deep, reaching to very slightly below the elbow. A true barrel chest is certainly not required, for this is more akin to the construction of the Pekingese and gives the dog a rolling action. Regarding depth of chest, the American Standard stipulates quite clearly that the ribcage should extend to just below the elbow.

The underline of the Shih Tzu should be pretty much parallel with the line of the back, without any accentuated tuck-up at the loin which is untypical of the breed. The coupling is the section between the back and front assemblies (from the rearmost point to the ribcage) and by "well coupled" we are effectively looking for a reasonably short coupling.

The shoulders of the Shih Tzu should be firm (but not loaded), and the muscle throughout should be in hard condition giving that sturdiness which is required by the Standard. There should be no roach on the back for, as mentioned with reference to the short upper arm, we are aiming for a level back and, indeed, a level topline.

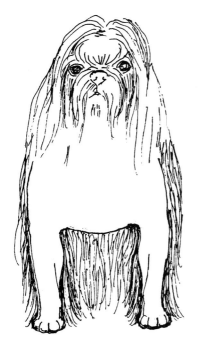

Correct.

Out at elbow, feet turned in.

*Out at
shoulder,
turned out
feet.*

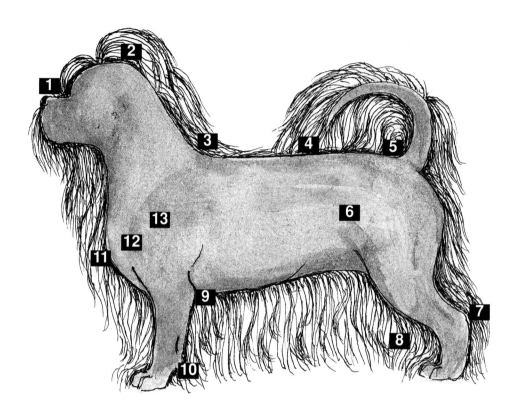

Anatomy of the Shih Tzu

1. Stop
2. Occiput
3. Withers
4. Level top-line
5. Root of tail

6. Coupling
7. Hock
8. Stifle
9. Elbow
10. Pastern

11. Sternum
12. Point of shoulder
13. Shoulder

TAIL

I feel that we should look at the tail before moving on to the hindquarters, for this is another feature of the dog which can be used to hide sins. All too frequently, I have observed a splendidly furnished tail draped carefully over an appalling topline. Of course, we all want to show off our dogs to their best advantage, but there is a danger, I feel, in believing that a fault such as this can be concealed and not paying sufficient attention to the problem in your breeding programme. A good judge will always assess the level of the back and the topline beneath the tail furnishings and, in any event, even the most heavily-coated tail cannot disguise the problem on the move. It is also important to bear in mind that a poor topline is usually indicative of other faults which give rise to it.

The tail should be high-set and should be in balance with the head. This means that a tail which lies flat to the back is uncharacteristic, as is one which is too low-set. It should be carried like a pot-handle, or, as accurately described in the American Standard "in a curve well over back", and should not be too tightly curled, for this will also destroy the balance of the outline. The Standard calls for the tail to be well feathered and, it goes without saying, that such feathering goes a long way to complete an attractive overall picture.

HINDQUARTERS AND FEET

We are still looking for muscle in the hindquarters and the Standard calls for short back legs to balance, of course, with the front ones. They should be straight when viewed from the rear, meaning that there should be no cow hocks and no bowing out. The use of the word straight in the Standard does not, however, mean in any way that the Shih Tzu should be straight in stifle. It requires some bend here, for straight stifles give a stilted action. Thighs should be well rounded.

As with the forefeet, the hindfeet should point neither in nor out, and all four feet should be rounded, firm and well-padded. They should be covered with plenty of hair and look larger than they actually are, once again adding to the sturdy appearance of the breed. The American Standard includes the sentence: "Angulation of hindquarters should be in balance with forequarters." This is hopefully taken as read when digesting the British Standard. However, it is good that the Americans take the trouble to point out this fundamental but highly important requirement.

GAIT AND MOVEMENT

Discussing the fore and hindquarters of the breed gives an indication of the type of movement which is characteristic. The front legs should reach well forward and this has, of necessity, to be coupled with a strong rear action which in the case of the Shih Tzu (but not the Lhasa Apso) shows the full pad when viewed from behind. The movement should be smooth-flowing, often likened to that of a ship in full sail, and the arrogance of the breed should be displayed also in its movement. If the neck and head carriage is correct, the Shih Tzu should be able to move with its head held high, without the necessity of stringing the dog up from the neck by its lead – the American Standard includes a clear statement that it should be "neither raced nor strung up". This stringing up of breeds is becoming all too common and plays havoc with the movement! A well balanced Shih Tzu, moving smoothly and with both head and tail held high, is a joy to watch.

COAT AND COLOUR

The coat on the Shih Tzu is not only to be long, but also dense with a good undercoat, and though a slight wave is permissible a curly coat is to be avoided. Texture is not mentioned in the Breed Standard and varies to a considerable extent according to coat colour. The hair on the head is tied in a top-knot and there should be ample furnishings on the tail and ears and, as has been mentioned, plenty of hair on the feet.

The Breed Standard permits all colours and interestingly also allows liver, as can be seen from the comments regarding liver pigmentation on the nose. (This is a colour which is also produced in the Lhasa Apso but is not permitted in the show-ring.) In parti-coloured dogs a white marking on the forehead (preferably central) and a white tip to the tail are highly desirable, as mentioned in the British and FCI Standards, but there is no mention of this in the American Standard.

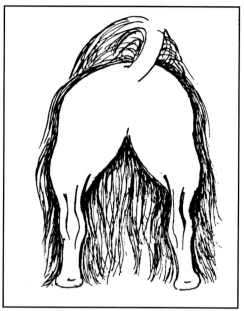

Correct hindquarters, viewed from the rear.

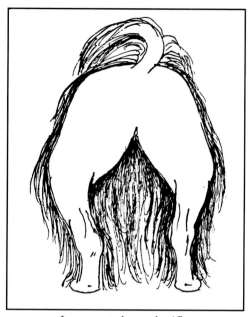

Incorrect: bowed stifles.

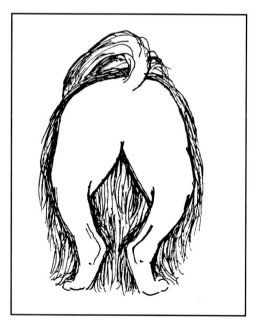

Incorrect: cow hocks.

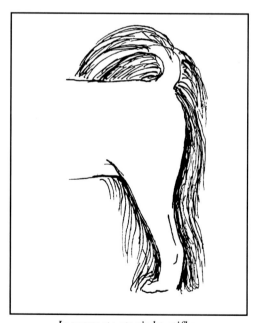

Incorrect: straight stifles.

WEIGHT AND SIZE

The Shih Tzu is heavy for its size and someone who is unfamiliar with the breed can be in for quite a shock when picking one up. The weight range given in the Standard is very wide indeed, even when taking into consideration the "ideal weight" of between 4.5 and 7.3 kg. (10 and 16lb.) in the British Standard. The American Standard asks for an ideal weight of between 9lb.-16lb. for mature dogs. Proportions are important and although the height specified is "not more than 26.7 cm (10$\frac{1}{2}$in.) this is qualified by the statement that "type and breed characteristics are not to be sacrificed to size alone". In the American Standard the ideal height is given as 9 to 10$\frac{1}{2}$in. Indeed, history has shown us that there has always been a certain dispute about size and, thus, the differences we find today are perhaps only to be expected.

To sum up, let us look at the key words in the Breed Standard clauses regarding GENERAL APPEARANCE, CHARACTERISTICS AND TEMPERAMENT. I would venture to suggest that readers study each one of the following words and phrases and then put them together to form a complete picture, bearing in mind the comments that I have made above:-

Sturdy.

Abundantly coated.

Distinctly arrogant carriage.

Chrysanthemum-like face.

Intelligent.

Active.

Alert.

Friendly.

Independent.

And there you have it – the Shih Tzu!

Chapter Six

SELECTING A PUPPY

Given that you are perfectly sure a Shih Tzu is really the dog for you, you will need to give much thought and planning as to how, when and from where you are going to obtain your puppy. The breed has, over the years, become very popular. There can be certain advantages to a breed's growth in popularity but there can be disadvantages too. As in any breed, there are those who breed dogs purely to make a profit and not for the good of the breed at all. The more popular breeds are even more susceptible to these type of people than the less well-known ones, for dealers are often prepared to buy entire litters, either to be sold through pet shops or, in some cases, via the export market. Many people who dispose of their puppies in such a way have not given serious thought to their breeding programmes, having simply mated together two dogs of the same breed which will, they hope, produce a litter of live puppies which can be off-loaded at the earliest possible opportunity. Some such puppies may be well nourished and cared for, but many are not. Put yourself, for a moment, in the position of a breeder. Would you be content to bring a litter of puppies into this world and let them go, eventually, to an unknown destination to people you had not met personally or about whom you had obtained excellent references? I think not.

I am sorry to begin this chapter on such a pessimistic note, but I feel it important that as a prospective Shih Tzu owner you should be aware of some of the less reputable breeding which goes on so that you can avoid those involved for motives other than the overall good of the breed. I know it is tempting to want to 'rescue' a puppy from the pet shop or from the unsavoury conditions in which you may have come across it but, unfortunately, buying from these sources only encourages such people to breed more. Once they have sold that particular litter it can be virtually guaranteed that they will breed yet another, and another! The motto is – buy from a reputable breeder. My intention here is to tell you how to find one. You may have decided that you wish to have a Shih Tzu as a pet or you may perhaps have aspirations in the show ring and would therefore like to buy one of potential show quality. Whatever your requirement, you will wish to buy a true and typical representative of the breed; one which has been well bred and well reared and is sound both in body and mind. It is important that the breeder from whom you purchase your puppy will be ready to give advice should ever you need to seek it.

It may well be that your first introduction to the breed was through someone who already owns a Shih Tzu or who has perhaps bred litters. This person may be able to point you in the right direction. Should this not be the case, you would probably be best advised to telephone the Hon. Secretary of one or more of the breed clubs and ask for telephone numbers of reputable breeders; if you are fortunate, you may also be able to find out which have puppies available for sale at the time of your enquiry. The telephone numbers of breed club secretaries can be obtained from the national Kennel Club. You may also find the occasional advertisement in the dog press, but I would urge you to be careful from whom you buy and certainly don't accept a puppy if the voice on the other end of the telephone offers to meet you half-way. This probably means that conditions at the kennels are not all they should be.

When you speak to breeders on the telephone make it perfectly clear whether you want a Shih Tzu to show or as a pet. Don't say that you intend to exhibit if you do not, for the breeder will not be at all happy to part with what they consider to be a potential show dog, only to find later that you had no intention of showing it at all, but just said that you did in order to obtain a good specimen. If you buy from a reputable breeder, the puppies which go as pets will have been brought up just as carefully as those destined to go to show homes. A word of caution for those of you who are looking for a puppy which you intend to show – beware of those who sell puppies as 'show puppies'. What a puppy probably has is show potential. It is simply not possible to say that a puppy of only a few weeks old will make a successful show dog, for it may not develop in the way you might have hoped; the positioning of the teeth and jaw may be wrong, the chest may not 'drop' to sufficient depth, the legs may grow longer than is desirable or the coat may not turn out to be of the correct quality or density. Sadly so much can go wrong and the younger the puppy you buy, the greater the risk you take.

If you are looking for a puppy for the show ring you would be wise to go along to at least a couple of shows in order to get into conversation with breeders and to take a close look at the Shih Tzu which are being exhibited. In this way you will probably be able to form an assessment of the type of breeding which most appeals to you. Breed Club Open or Championship Shows or General (all breeds) Championship Shows are the ones you should visit, for at these you will find a large number of exhibits, and possibly a fairly wide cross-section of bloodlines. If you just go along to your local Open Show, the chances are that you will only find a handful of exhibitors who live in your own general area, and the stock you see may not be truly representative of the breed. I cannot stress enough that if you want a Shih Tzu which you can proudly take into the show ring and which, hopefully, will do a fair amount of winning, you must select both the puppy and the breeder with care. Most breeders with sufficient experience will have a reasonably good eye for selecting puppies with show potential, and they would not wish to sell a puppy which they felt would not do their breeding justice in the ring. After all, the puppy will carry the breeder's affix and therefore it is to that person's advantage to sell one with potential rather than one which will rarely be placed in the cards at shows. An experienced breeder will also be able to give advice, not only about the general up-bringing of your new puppy but they will also be able to give guidance as to which judges are likely to appreciate the merits of her stock. Sound advice of this kind could save you many long, expensive and fruitless journeys to

Jardhu King Kole and Jardhu Koffee Kream, pictured at the delightful age of four months.

David J. Lindsay.

Left to right: Dusky Rose of Bellakerne, Bellakerne Misty-Do, Tamanu Triska of Bellakerne (at five months) and Bellakerne Liza-Do. Despite the vast difference in coat colour, all are related.   *Photo by Carol Ann Johnson.*

exhibit under judges who, because they have a different understanding of the Breed Standard, tend to select stock which differs greatly from that which you are exhibiting.

Sooner or later you will have made an appointment to visit a breeder and to look at the puppies that are available. All good breeders should be willing to show you the puppies' dam, though you should bear in mind that she will probably not be looking her best having reared a litter of hungry puppies and her coat may well not resemble its former glory! Nonetheless, she should be clean and should look in healthy condition. Depending on the age of the puppies when you go to see them, you may or may not be allowed to touch them, in any event it is to be hoped that the breeder will have had the good sense to ask you to wash your hands thoroughly as some measure of precaution against passing on infections, especially in the case of young puppies who have not begun their vaccination programmes. In some cases the sire of the puppies will be available for you to see, but he may well belong to another owner. However, if you arrive at a house and find more than one litter running together, and the breeder does not appear to know which puppies belong to which dam, you should treat this situation with extreme suspicion. It has been known for breeders to issue the wrong pedigrees with puppies, in some cases because two litters have been born within a few days of each other and the puppies have been mixed up. It goes without saying that if this has happened the breeder has not exercised sufficient care and, naturally, an incorrect pedigree will play havoc in any future breeding which goes on from the lines involved.

If you are seeking a show puppy you will most probably have to be guided by the experience of the breeder as to which puppy is the most suitable for you. It would be helpful to take along a friend who already has substantial experience within the breed or, if this is not possible, someone who is well acquainted with one of the other relatively small breeds and has already had experience in selecting young stock with show potential. On the other hand, if you are seeking a family pet, you should select the puppy which appeals to you most. In this case, personality will probably play the most important part in your selection and so, possibly, will coat pattern and coat colour, though this should certainly not be the sole reason for your final decision. The Breed Standard gives no colour preference, other than stating that a white blaze is desirable in parti-colours. On the subject of coat, do bear in mind that if you are looking at a young puppy its coat will be much, much shorter than when it is adult. A good indicator of quantity and density of coat when mature is to look at the coat on the tummy. If there is plenty of it, not necessarily in length but in density, this is a promising sign for the future.

Under no circumstances should you buy a puppy which is offered for sale under the age of eight weeks, and if you are buying one for the show ring you may find that the breeder will not part with it until around twenty weeks. By then the breeder will have a clearer idea of whether or not it really will be suitable for exhibition purposes. I am afraid that there is always a risk that even after what seems like an endless wait, you may still fail to find the puppy you had hoped for because something has 'gone wrong'. Disappointing though this may be, you would be better advised to wait a while longer for something really special, rather than take home a puppy of inferior quality which will not do well in the ring.

When agreeing to purchase a Shih Tzu puppy, be sure that you are fully aware of the terms of the contract between you and the breeder. Do not get caught up in breeding agreements unless you are sure that you really want to be involved in breeding. If a breeding agreement is reached, which normally means that you will be obliged to mate your bitch to a stud dog of the bitch's breeder's choosing, and return one or more puppies to her, only agree to this if everything is clearly set down in writing so that there is no chance of disagreement later on. Is there a certain age by which the bitch must be mated? What happens if the bitch is mated but does not produce puppies? At what stage are the registration papers be passed over to you? (The latter can affect whether or not you are the registered breeder of the resultant litter of puppies.) If the bitch's breeder is to take back one or more puppies, is she to have first pick from the litter? If she requests, for example, two bitch puppies and your bitch's litter only produces one bitch, will you be obliged to mate her again and, if so, will that be to the same stud dog? Most importantly, no-one should ever agree to breeding terms unless the Shih Tzu they have bought is of good enough quality to breed from and, in my personal opinion, no bitch should be bred from unless she is worthy of entry in competition at Championship Shows. I would therefore be very dubious about any breeding terms offered on a bitch which is being purchased at between eight and twelve weeks and destined simply to be a much-loved family pet.

When you go along to purchase your puppy there will be many questions which you will wish to ask but which you may not think of on the spur of the moment, so it is a good idea to jot down your questions on a piece of paper so that you don't forget anything. Ask the breeder if the puppy has, or is likely to develop, any hereditary defects. An umbilical hernia, for example, can occasionally be present and the breeder should be able to inform you about this. It would also be wise to agree that the puppy goes to a vet for a check-up, which should be done immediately so that if there is a problem which needs to be sorted out, there is no delay on either part. Check whether or not the puppy is registered with the Kennel Club and, if so, whether there are any endorsements on the registration, such as that a bitch may not be bred from or a dog not be used at stud. You should certainly be given a pedigree when you take the puppy home, and this must bear the breeder's signature certifying its authenticity.

I do feel that all those who sell Shih Tzu puppies should offer to give a brief grooming demonstration to new owners of the breed; this can be done when the puppy is purchased. Hopefully your tiny puppy will already have been introduced to a brush and will, if you are lucky or are buying a slightly older puppy for the show ring, have been taught to lie over on its side so that it may be groomed. You should be shown how to care for nails and should be advised whether or not dewclaws have been left on, for if they have, you will need to pay a little extra attention when grooming around the feet. Because the Shih Tzu is such a long-coated breed, it usually grows a great deal of hair in the ear. This can be plucked out easily, and it will be of invaluable assistance if the breeder can demonstrate how to do this, as extreme care must be taken not to damage the ear or to probe too far inside.

At the time of purchase the breeder must advise you of the worming programme which has been carried out or is already underway. The breeder will probably be able to provide you with a tablet for the next worming session but, if not, you should obtain suitable worming tablets from your vet rather than buy them over the counter at a pet shop. Depending on the age of your puppy and also taking into account the type of vaccine used by the breeder's vet, your puppy's vaccination programme may or may not have commenced. It is essential that you are perfectly clear about this, and that a relevant vaccination certificate is passed on to you if injections have been given. This will provide essential information for your own vet. Additionally you will require a diet sheet for your new puppy. Naturally, you will be at liberty to change the diet and, of course, to increase the quantity of food given as the weeks progress, but in the early stages it is essential that the puppy is fed just as it has been in its previous home. The pup will have sufficient to adjust to in its new environment, without its dam and littermates, so consistency in its diet is important. Personally, I always send my own puppies away with a little package of the foods they will need to keep them going for the next few days, for there is always the danger that the new owner's local pet shop does not stock quite the same brand of food that I have been feeding. If your puppy's breeder does not offer this, it might be a good idea to ask if you might pay for a small supply, just to be on the safe side.

TRAVELLING HOME

When you go to collect your puppy take along a plentiful supply of soft white kitchen towelling and a couple of towels, for there is a chance that your precious little youngster will not be a good traveller at first. The puppy will most probably learn to overcome its travelling discomforts with a little experience and, if it does not, there are some excellent canine travel-sickness tablets available for sale from pet shops, stalls at dog shows and from veterinary surgeries. However, your new puppy will probably be a little too young for a tablet on its first journey home. It will feel most comfortable sitting on your lap with your arms clasped gently around it, so that it feels secure. Always try to take a companion along with you when collecting your puppy so that the journey home will be easier. If this is not possible, you cannot, of course, drive with the little fellow on your lap so take along a fairly small, deep-sided, cardboard box, padded on the bottom with something practical and yet very comfortable. A thick base lining of newspaper, with a piece of veterinary bedding and a towel on top of would be ideal, for the towel can be removed and replaced easily in case of accident. The box must, of necessity be firmly wedged in the car so that it does not slide about during the journey home.

ARRIVING HOME

Try to arrange to collect your new-found friend at a time which enables you to return home during the day or in the early evening. In this way you will have a good few hours to accustom the puppy to its new surroundings before everyone turns in for the night. Of course, the puppy will find things strange at first so do not be surprised if it does not appear to be the happy, bumptious little fellow it appeared in the more familiar surroundings of the breeder's home. The puppy will be tired, but probably unwilling to sleep because of the new environment. It is not unusual for a puppy to refuse food on its first night away from home, but you should be able to get it to take a little something by the second day. Make sure, however, that it has sufficient liquid, even if it means just moistening its lips that very first night.

The puppy's first night at home is not the time to invite all your neighbours and your children's school friends around to play with the newcomer. Please give your puppy time to settle in, and to get to know its new family. In the early stages it will be very important that it gets to know your voices, and you should not be too rough with it. It will probably seek out a certain pair of feet next to which it can curl up and settle down, much to the chagrin of the owners of the other pairs of feet which have not been selected! If the puppy wishes to settle down and sleep, let it do so; there will plenty of time for playing in the days ahead. It will probably have had quite a busy time at its old home with all the excitement of your visit, and the car journey may have been tiring, so the pup may well feel that a rest is in order. It is only a youngster and its own body will dictate how much it can take at any one time. Indeed, you will probably be surprised at just how much puppies do sleep in the early months of their lives.

You will have to appreciate that although your puppy may be semi-house-trained, it will not know where it is meant to do its toilet in its new home. There should be an escape-proof area of your garden or terrace designated especially for the puppy and, for the sake of safety while vaccinations are still in progress, no other dogs should have access to it. Newspaper should, however, be accessible in its sleeping quarters during the first few days. My personal advice is that you provide newspaper by the door so that when it does start to realise that it has to ask at the door to be let out, it is not caught short if you happen not to be there in time. It is far better for the puppy to have an accident on newspaper than on your sitting room carpet! Always be sure to clean up immediately after your puppy, and this also applies in the garden. Just a few puppies (of any breed) have some rather unsavoury habits, so it is far better to keep temptation out of their way, apart from the fact that if you are the owner of a dog, scrupulous cleanliness is a must.

Your new puppy must have a bed of its own, preferably somewhere out of the way where it can relax without disturbance, but it will most probably appreciate its bed being positioned somewhere where it can see you, or at least have an idea of what is going on around it. Shih Tzu undoubtedly prefer to live in the home and, being essentially clean and convivial dogs, this rarely causes any problem. Sleeping quarters should always be be thoroughly dry and away from draughts, and for this reason the bed should be positioned a couple of inches from the ground. I would certainly not recommend one of the rather attractive looking wicker baskets because puppies, and indeed grown dogs, are prone to chew them and they can very easily catch the long and precious coat of your Shih Tzu, added to which they are not at all easy to keep clean. There are some exceptionally strong plastic kidney shaped boxes on the market at most major outlets, and these suit admirably well and can be hosed down for thorough cleaning when necessary. Your Shih Tzu should, of course, be provided with a comfortable lining in the base. Whether or not you allow your dog to have full access to your furniture entirely depends on you, but you must start as you mean to go on. It is absolutely no use allowing your puppy on the sofa one day and not the next, for you will do nothing more than confuse it. If it is only allowed to stay at ground floor level, that is the way it must be from day one. If you have no objection to allowing your puppy on the furniture, it must be very carefully supervised at all times, especially while it is young. In the early months of its life it must never be allowed to jump from any great height for risk of injury, possibly resulting in permanent damage. Puppies are very quick and you should never forget that they are just as capable of leaping off the arm or back of the sofa as they are of going back down again in the direction from whence they came! For the same reason it is important not to leave a Shih Tzu alone on a grooming table, for a matter of three feet or so is a very great height for a small dog, more than three times a Shih Tzu's own height. If you think of that in human terms it may help you to appreciate the likely damage.

Hopefully you will not encounter too much difficulty in getting your Shih Tzu lead trained. Begin with a neatly fitting collar around its neck (always under supervision) just to get it used to the feel of it. Soon you will be able to add a clip-on lead, or a show lead can take the place of the collar for practice sessions, if you have a show puppy. I would, however, like to stress that it is most unwise to take any puppy out among traffic on a show lead for there is always the danger that it might pull back and slip its head out, leading to escape and possible tragedy. Until your puppy is about six months old it is not wise to over exercise a Shih Tzu. Short walks on a lead are quite sufficient for lead training. Any other exercise should be off the lead so that it can stop and rest whenever it feels a need to do so. If you have more than one dog at home you will probably be surprised at how much two dogs exercise one another, for they exercise all their muscles while twisting and turning in play. If, however, your other dog is substantially heavier than your puppy, never allow them to get too rough with one another. As adults Shih Tzu seem to hold their own perfectly well with the larger breeds, but it goes without saying that you must be entirely certain of the temperament of both if they are allowed to exercise together.

If you intend to keep your Shih Tzu in long coat every little twig must be removed from the coat when returning home, for if even the smallest burr is allowed to remain it will create a knot in the long coat. Look out for grass seeds, which can all too easily get lodged in the ears or nose and can even work their way into the skin, causing an abscess. Dogs should not be walked in extreme heat nor, of course, should they be left in cars, not even with the windows open on what appears to be only a mild day, for heat inside a car builds up all too quickly and the saddest accidents have occurred. If your Shih Tzu gets wet you will have to dry it off thoroughly immediately on returning home, and if it has been allowed out in the snow – something it is almost certain to love – you will find that hard little balls of snow have formed on its feet, up its legs and on the underside. The only way to remove these successfully is to stand the dog in a shallow bath of tepid water and rinse them off. If you leave them to melt, you will find that the ends of the coat will break when dry. A little oil on the coat before going out in the snow will help to prevent the snow from adhering. Although many Shih Tzu seem to adore a romp along the beach, and even in the sea, salt water is not good for the coat, and so it will have to be rinsed out afterwards. Take care also that the sand does not get into the dog's eyes and that there is no irritation to the skin.

If there is a cat in your household you will most probably find that once they have both learned to respect each other they will get on well enough. However, you will have to watch that your cat does not scratch the eyes of your Shih Tzu, which are especially vulnerable as not only are they prominent, but the coat is tied up exposing them still further. Usually your dog will be quick enough to get out of the way should a set of claws aim in its direction, but if the eye is caught urgent veterinary attention is essential. Any sign of blueness in the eye may well be an indication that the eye was scratched a day or so ago so, again, get your Shih Tzu to the vet immediately.

The Shih Tzu is a breed which is fond of human companionship and it is unlikely that your dog will take a dislike to any particular member of the family, provided, of course, that it is well treated by all. Many, though, do seem to bestow their affections especially on one person, often the one which the dog connects with exercise and food! If there are young children in the home they must be taught to be sensible with the dog, more especially so because it is relatively small and has a long coat. It is awfully tempting for a child to pull at the coat or to create different hair styles, neither of which should be encouraged for both can be painful and the latter may spell doom if you have a show dog on which you wish to preserve every hair!

Hopefully your young puppy will have no sign of worms because the breeder followed a routine worming programme which you will have to continue. If you are unfortunate enough to purchase a Shih Tzu which is suffering in this way its appetite will probably be spasmodic, and its coat will be lacking in sheen. It may also have a runny nose and eyes, a cough and possibly a pot-belly (especially in a young puppy). Roundworms can either be passed in the motions or in severe cases can be vomited. It is worth mentioning that it is unwise to worm a dog when it is ill from another cause, so do be sure that worms really are the problem before you begin worming treatment. Tapeworms, consisting of segments which can be passed in the motions, are less likely to occur in a dog but you should be on the alert, especially if you live in a farming area and if your dog exercises where sheep have grazed. One of the intermediate hosts of the tapeworm is the flea and so it is imperative that your canine companion is kept free from this type of infestation. With a bit of luck you will never even see a flea on your dog, but if you do so, don't be too alarmed. Even the cleanest animal can be selected by this intelligent little creature, and there is always a risk that your own meticulously clean Shih Tzu might have come into contact with a dog which is carrying fleas. Use of an anti-parasitic shampoo is usually very effective, but it is always sensible also to keep a tin of flea spray in the cupboard; this can be used not only on the dog but also on bedding and carpeting. Avoid spraying into the eyes, nostrils or ears, and read the manufacturer's instructions very carefully, for such sprays should not be used on very young puppies and a minimum age limit will usually be specified.

Your Shih Tzu's teeth will need to be kept in good order and it is far better to look after this aspect of general health yourself than to let plaque and tartar build up on the teeth so that the vet has to give an anaesthetic in order to clean them up again. Some Shih Tzu are rather late teethers and may well not have cut their second set of teeth until the age of five or six months. Do not trouble your dog with tooth cleaning equipment while the gums are still sore from teething, but when you are happy that your Shih Tzu is no longer suffering any discomfort in the mouth you can apply a canine toothpaste or even just a cloth dipped in a 1 to 10 bicarbonate of soda solution. Tooth scalers are also available, but I would not recommend that these are used by the novice unless expert advice has been given. At regular intervals give your Shih Tzu a hard biscuit to chew on; this helps to keep both teeth and gums in good condition. I do not like bones to be given unless they are marrow bones and, as these are really too large for a Shih Tzu, my personal advice would be to avoid bones altogether and let hard biscuits and a little personal care keep your dog's teeth in good order.

Because of the long coat there is always a chance that your Shih Tzu will get a dirty bottom occasionally, actually this happens with more frequency when your dog is not thoroughly groomed out. A change of diet, possibly a different make of food from usual or a surfeit of biscuits at bed-time, can easily be a cause. Deal with the problem as soon as it is noticed for it must be very uncomfortable, and if it is not attended to it can cause soreness. Your dog will usually realize that you are trying to help, and I find it easiest to sit the dog on the edge of the sink, washing with my right hand and the dog firmly supported in my left, thus avoiding getting its legs wet. Not the most pleasant task in the world, but one with which you will have to put up if you have chosen to have a small long-coated breed!

On your visits to the vet for vaccinations do not put your puppy down on the floor, for if its vaccination programme is not complete it will be susceptible to contracting disease. Neither should you let the puppy come into direct contact with the other dogs in the surgery, and you will, I am afraid, have to politely discourage other owners from stroking the pup when it is on your knee. People are all too fond of making a bee-line for young puppies without considering what their own dog might be suffering from. Vets' surgeries should always be spotlessly clean, but it is also wise just to check that the examination table has been wiped over before you place your puppy on it. The vet will most probably expect you to hold your puppy steady while he injects, so if you are likely to turn into a squirming wreck at the sight of a needle, advise him of this from the outset so that he can get a nurse to assist. When the course of injections is complete do be sure to wait the full amount of time stipulated by your vet before you take your puppy out where it will come into contact with other dogs. Recommendations vary according to the vaccine used. Most vets do not commence the vaccination programme until at least ten weeks because every puppy carries a certain amount of immunity from its dam, and if it is injected too early the vaccine may not be effective.

Although Shih Tzu are perhaps happiest in the home they can be kennelled outdoors if absolutely necessary, and usually this is only the case if you have a substantial number of dogs. In such circumstances it is essential that they have sufficient to occupy their attention, and so the kennel should be sighted near to the house so that they can both see and hear activity around them. Naturally, a kennelled Shih Tzu should be given plenty of human attention and will appreciate some time in the house even if it sleeps outside at night. Kennelling is much a matter of fancy and will depend on a number of factors, but it goes without saying that it must be dry, clean, raised slightly from the ground and that it should be sufficiently warm in winter. Take care that both kennel and run have some protection from strong summer sun so that dogs are not trapped in heat from which they have no escape. Shih Tzu can frequently be kept together in small numbers without in-fighting although, as with all breeds, a bitch's temperament can change around the time of her season and she may need to be separated from one or more of her female companions, as well as from any male dogs with which she usually keeps company. I am always dubious about keeping stud dogs together, but there are certainly some who seem to get on well with one another, though I would always recommend that caution is exercised at all times. It is clear that bitches and dogs must be kept well apart when the former are in season, but I would urge you not to underestimate the ability of some of the young dogs. Males as little as six months old have been known to mate bitches when their owners thought there was no danger, and bitches are also capable of conceiving even when mated at their first season though, mercifully, accidents involving young bitches seem to occur with less frequency.

Chapter Seven

COAT CARE AND GROOMING

The Shih Tzu is long coated breed, added to which it has undercoat and is quite low to the ground. These three important facts mean that to keep a Shih Tzu in full coat involves a considerable amount of work. Allow your Shih Tzu to get severely matted and you will simply have much more work to do when bath-time finally comes around. If its coat gets in really bad condition you will probably end up putting the scissors to the coat, something you perhaps didn't plan to do – and a short coat takes quite a while to grow again! It is, of course, possible to keep a pet Shih Tzu in short coat, and there is certainly no shame in this. It is far better for a dog to be clipped short and feel comfortable than to have a long, densely matted coat which must feel highly irritating, probably smells, and runs a greater risk of harbouring parasites. But grooming a Shih Tzu is not all doom and gloom. The time spent bathing and grooming your dog can be an important time for a bond to build up between you; it is time to be alone with your canine friend, and I rather think others would be surprised how many of our intimate secrets we impart to our canine companions at bath-time.

We have already touched on training your puppy to lie over for short grooming sessions, even from a very young age and, in adulthood, when the coat has developed both in length and in density, taking longer both to dry and to groom out thoroughly, you will be glad that you trained your youngster to behave well on the table. It is not possible to give hard and fast rules about which is the best way to groom, for everyone has their own little habits and slightly differing techniques, and you are sure to discover your own preferences in time. The frequency with which you need to bath your Shih Tzu will vary not only according to whether it is a household pet or a show dog, but also according to the texture and, to a certain extent, colour of its coat. Different colours do tend to have slightly differing textures. Some coats appear to hold the dirt more than others, and others need more time to settle following a bath; such dogs look better in the show-ring if they have been bathed a couple of days prior to the show rather than the night

Ch. Kareth Kismet of Lyre (Ch. Firefox of Santosha – Kareth Khamelion). Photographed at six months, Kismet was then in full puppy coat. *David J. Lindsay.*

before. It has also to be said that there are breeders who never bath their dogs completely at all, perhaps just freshening up feet and underparts. Their view is that bathing takes the natural oil out of the coat but, from a personal point of view, on the rare occasions that I have taken a dog to a show without a bath, I have never felt it to be perfectly clean.

Whatever is your chosen method of dealing with the coat, in the show ring presentation is of great importance (sometimes more important than it should be!) and even the most soundly constructed and otherwise typical Shih Tzu can be ruined by an ill-prepared coat which, for the judge, is unpleasant not only to look at but also to touch. Such inconsiderate presentation is not by any means prevalent in the breed, but I have come across it from time to time and it seems such a dreadful pity!

TOOLS FOR GROOMING

The tools you will require to groom your Shih Tzu will be virtually the same whether it is to be kept as a pet or as a show dog. Some articles of equipment are quite expensive, but they will give you many years of good service and will aid you in the grooming process, speeding up the operation slightly and giving a better finish to the coat. Much of the equipment can be purchased at good pet stores (particularly if the owners are involved with dogs and dog showing) but for items such as grooming tables and hair-dryers, and for the best selection of equipment available, you should visit one of the major General Championship Shows where there is a whole host of stalls selling every imaginable sort of canine equipment. If you are planning on buying a puppy for the show ring you will hopefully be visiting such shows before you do so, and even if you have no real interest in shows but want a Shih Tzu as a pet, you will probably find that at some time during the year there is a Championship Show reasonably near to your home. Alternatively, you may like to make a special visit to Crufts at the National Exhibition Centre near Birmingham, but beware of becoming overwhelmed and confused by all the different products available for sale! In offering the following list of equipment may I make it clear that slightly different tools and products seem to suit various coat textures and, as I have said before, personal preference will, naturally, play a part in your final selection.

BRUSH: In my own opinion a pure bristle brush, with the bristles bedded in a soft cushioning, is the most suitable, though some owners prefer the brush to be a mixture of nylon and bristle. A simple wire brush is totally unsuitable for it will drag out far too much coat and can catch the dog's skin. Some exhibitors use a good quality wire brush with coated ends, though this is generally only used for finishing.

COMBS: A steel comb with both medium and wide teeth is arguably the best and can be used for finishing and for teasing out knots. A fine-toothed comb can be used with extreme caution on difficult little areas such as around the teats, under the 'armpits' and for removing small particles of food from the beard.

SHAMPOO: There is an enormous variety of canine shampoos on the market and you should choose that which you feel will best suit your own dog's coat. Some exhibitors like to use one of the mild insecticidal shampoos, not only as a precaution against parasites but also because they tend not to soften the coat too much. Many owners like to use a human baby shampoo on the head, and this is also suitable when bathing tiny youngsters so as not to aggravate their delicate skin.

CONDITIONER: There is almost as great a range of conditioners available as there is shampoos. Which one you select is much a matter of preference and the texture of your own dog's coat will play an important part in your final choice.

SCISSORS: You will certainly need a good sharp pair of canine or human hairdressing scissors for use when trimming feet. Some of the trade stands at dog shows offer a sharpening service.

NAIL CLIPPERS: You can, of course, have your Shih Tzu's claws cut by the vet if you wish, but nail trimming is a simple procedure and you would be well advised to get into the habit of doing it yourself. There are two types of clipper, guillotine and straight edged; I personally find the former easier to use.

EAR TWEEZERS: As the Shih Tzu is a long coated breed, hair will grow inside the ears and if left there is an added risk that wax and consequent infection can build up inside the ear canal. Good quality ear tweezers, which must have blunt ends and ideally a 'scissor hold' for your fingers, are easy to use and cause the dog no pain, although it is essential that you do not delve too deeply into the ear.

GROOMING TABLE: This needs to be waist high and with a non-slip surface, it must also be perfectly stable so that your Shih Tzu feels thoroughly confident when standing on it. Various types can be purchased from dog shows, perhaps the most practical of which fold down and can be pulled along for use as a trolley for wheeling your dog crate into the show-ground. These are, however, rather heavy. There is also now a crate on wheels, with a grooming table surface attached. These look highly practical, but they may not be suitable for use at all shows as the crates cannot always be dismantled for use on the show-bench. Your grooming table will be one of the most expensive items of equipment so select it with care. If you have a pet Shih Tzu you will most probably be able to make do with an old kitchen table, and simply attach a piece of rubber matting to the surface.

TOWELS: You will need at least one good-sized towel for wrapping your dog when it comes out of the bath, and a couple of smaller ones for dealing with wet feet.

ELASTICS: 'Dental elastics' are tiny elastic bands which are used to tie up the Shih Tzu's head furnishings. These can be obtained from good pet shops and from stalls at dog shows.

CONDITIONING SPRAY: A conditioning spray is useful for finishing off the coat after bathing and before taking your exhibit into the show-ring. However, there is a Kennel Club rule precluding exhibitors from altering the texture of the coat, so take care when purchasing a conditioner that it is not one which contravenes KC rules.

HAIR-DRYER: I have left this until last, for if you decide to buy a professional canine hair-dryer this will almost certainly be your most expensive piece of equipment. Of course, if you have only one pet Shih Tzu you may be able to manage perfectly well with a human-type, hand-held dryer – perhaps a useful handyman can erect a stand for it so that it can perch safely somewhere near the grooming table while you are drying. However, if you have a show dog and especially if you have a number of long-haired dogs, I feel that a proper dryer is indispensable. There is a wide variety of types available, some table-top models and some which stand on the floor. Most have a variety of speeds, blowing hot, medium or cold air. When you use such a dryer not only will you have both hands free for grooming, but you will also be able to adjust the height and angle of the flow, and you will almost certainly be able to get a better finish on the coat than you otherwise would. Canine hair-dryers are available from General Championship Shows and a few can be obtained by mail order. I would, however, caution you to buy any necessary spares which are recommended, for although you may not need them for a long while you can guarantee that when a small part such as a washer does fail, it will be the night before an important show. Because good dryers last for many years – my own is at least fifteen years old and still going strong – there is the danger that when you need spare parts the models have changed and the parts need to be specially ordered – this has happened to me and I have had to wait a long time, so I now make sure that I am always well prepared for any eventuality.

USEFUL TIPS
1. Give your dog ample opportunity to relieve itself before bathing or before any lengthy grooming session. This prevents the dog becoming uncomfortable while on the grooming table, and it will most probably be more relaxed and therefore better behaved.
2. Never leave a dog on a table unattended – however well behaved, it is all too easy for the dog to become distracted and to jump off causing injury.
3. Never groom the coat when it is absolutely dry, for this will cause breakage to the ends of the hair. Grooming dry also tends to remove more coat than would otherwise be necessary. Even if you are grooming immediately before a bath, always use conditioning spray or, if you prefer, water dispensed from a fine-spray bottle.

Tying up the top-knot: carefully draw the head furnishings back before drawing over the elastic.

Photo by Carol Ann Johnson.

HEAD AND TOP-KNOT

The head is a very important feature of the Shih Tzu and if you wish your dog to look its best you will need to learn how to keep eyes and whiskers thoroughly clean and to tie the top-knot to best advantage. The eyes of the Shih Tzu are fairly large and, especially with the hair tied up, can be exposed to damage so do check them every day. The eyes and the area around them can be bathed in one of the special canine liquid eye cleaners or in Optrex. Always take extreme care when removing matts from around the eye for it is not difficult to take out too much of the coat, leaving a bare and possibly sore patch below the eye. Beard and whiskers should be washed and combed through as regularly as necessary to keep them free from remnants of food. If you wish, you can attach an elastic on each side of the beard to help avoid soiling.

The hair on the ears needs to be brushed downwards and you will need to pay special attention to the area behind the ear where the coat is often of a much finer texture; this is particularly prone to matting. On no account should these matts be cut out but should be gently teased or brushed. A great many Shih Tzu seem to grow quite a substantial amount of hair inside the ear and this should be gently removed with your special tweezers. If you remove only two or three strands of hair with each pull you will find that the operation is quite painless. Do not attempt to remove a whole clump of hair at the same time, and do not delve too deeply with the tweezers.

From the age of about five months your puppy's head fall will be just about long enough to begin to tie up. Comb up the hair from the stop and fix into an elastic band, taking care not to

A correctly tied top-knot. *Photo by Carol Ann Johnson.*

pull up the hair too tightly so that it pulls on the eyes. When removing the elastic never pull it out but always cut through the band so as not to break any hairs. The top-knot of a show dog should never be trimmed, but some pet owners prefer to keep the head hair short so that it is more manageable. In such cases the hair can be allowed to fall over the eyes or can be clipped short as in a puppy.

Teeth will need to be checked and cleaned regularly so that no tartar is allowed to build up on them. As mentioned in the previous chapter, there are some dog toothpastes available which can be used either with a canine toothbrush or a piece of cloth wrapped around your finger. Alternatively, or as an additional measure, provided that you have had expert guidance, you may decide to scale the teeth from time to time when any signs of tartar appear. A canine 'de-scaler' is available from one or two stalls at General Championship Shows.

BODY COAT

When you have got your Shih Tzu to lie on its side on the grooming table, the coat should be parted and layered and brushed section by section, always in the direction of the coat growth so as not to take out too much hair. It is important to get right down to the skin for if you concentrate only on the top-coat the undercoat will remain in and will matt, giving a bulky appearance. Too much undercoat left in the coat will prevent the growth of new coat.

If you have to deal with a matt in the coat (and when all is said and done, some dogs do seem to develop matts overnight!) you should spray the matt itself with a generous helping of conditioner or anti-tangle spray, leave this for a few moments to soak in thoroughly and then gently tease out the matt with your fingers, always working from the inside out. Very tight knots may need to be teased out with the end of the wide-toothed section of a comb but never tug the comb through the knot for, this will not only hurt your dog, it will also take out far too much of the coat. If you have a show dog the coat should never get in such bad condition that you are unable to remove a matt by either of the above means, but, in extreme cases, if the tangle is so tight that it cannot even be removed with a comb, you will need to use scissors. Pointing the scissors outwards from the skin, snip through the centre of the knot; having split it in two you should find that you can work carefully away at each of the two sections in turn, with eventual success. But you must cut in the direction of the coat growth, if you cut across the coat or at an angle you will simply end up with a patch of short coat.

The tummy is quite tender so take especial care not to tug too hard in this area and, provided that you groom your Shih Tzu out regularly you should be able to manage only with your bristle brush, perhaps just checking through with a comb. If you ever need to trim the coat on the tummy do take extreme care not to cut through a nipple, and remember that dogs have nipples as well as bitches. The 'armpits', I find, seem especially prone to developing little knots so check them frequently. Rather than tug away at a tiny knot under the armpit, I have no worries about cutting little knots away from this area for it does not show at all and avoids the likelihood of them building up in the future. If you are grooming out without bathing it is wise to wipe over a dog's penis with a damp sponge to keep the area fresh, but do be sure that the coat is completely dry before he goes out into a cold atmosphere. On the tricky subject of penises, you can trim a little of the hair off the end (for sometimes there seems to be yards of it) but always leave at least a good half inch or so, for if you cut it any shorter the tiny hairs can aggravate the penis and set up an infection.

Ch. Sueman Shiatzu Chaz at Emrose refuses to lie over to be groomed. Despite this, his owner Julie Howells, presents him to perfection, aided by the fact that he is happy to sit up to be groomed.

Photo by Carol Ann Johnson.

LEGS AND FEET

The trousers of the Shih Tzu are heavily coated and you will always need to check that they are free of little bits of debris so as to avoid knots forming. The back legs may also benefit from a damp sponge if you have not bathed your dog, for there is always a risk of staining from urine. Shih Tzu like to be clean so always keep a careful eye on your dog's back end to see that nothing has stuck to its coat following its toilet. Any dirt should be removed immediately. Again, do see that the coat is thoroughly dried for not only is a damp coat uncomfortable but it will also cause the coat to curl.

Some dogs don't seem to mind having their feet groomed but others seem particularly sensitive in this area, which can be a real nuisance – so I hope you are lucky enough to have the former! Take care that the feet do not remain wet if your dog has been running on grass or has come in from wet ground, and be especially careful when grooming not to catch the comb in the dew claws if they have remained on. You will need to check regularly and carefully under the pads and to trim off the hair which grows beneath. If you allow this hair to remain it will build up into very hard little knots which get stuck tightly between the pads; these can cause a dog to go lame and they are rather tricky to cut out – so don't let them build up in the first place! Although the Shih Tzu is not a trimmed breed, most exhibitors do trim around the feet just slightly, for on some dogs the coat can grow so long that it spoils the outline and the dog can almost trip up on its coat on the move. The neatest way of cutting around the feet is to stand the dog on the edge of a table, making sure that it is at full stretch and not slumped, and trim to table height in the knowledge that you will not be trimming off too much but exactly to floor level.

Nails will need to be checked regularly, especially dewclaws which do not wear down naturally, as they have no contact with any surface. Those dogs which run on concrete are less likely to require regular nail trimming than those which spend most of their time in the garden or on carpet. Most dogs, given plenty of practice, accept nail trimming as part of the grooming process and lie on their side making your life perfectly easy. A few, however, seem to detest this particular little operation and try to be as awkward as they possibly can. These awkward few are probably best held on one person's lap while another sees to the nails, taking extreme care not to cut into the quick which would be very painful. On pale-coloured claws it is easy to see where the quick begins, but on dark-coloured nails avoiding the quick is pure guess-work, so just take a little off at a time to avoid damage. In the unfortunate event of cutting into the quick and causing it to bleed, a little touch of potassium permanganate will stem the flow.

When your dog has been thoroughly groomed out and you are certain that there is not a knot or tangle left in sight, you should stand it on the table and carefully make a parting down the centre of the back. You may like to use a grooming spray to put that finishing touch, but do be careful not to use too much or you will destroy the natural look of the coat. Unless the spray you are using is very fine, you may find it better to spray on to the palm on your hand and then gently brush your hands over the coat.

BATHING

If your bath has a slippery surface it would be wise to place a rubber mat in the bottom so that your dog feels secure and does not slip. It should be trained to stand where you put it and not to move about, for bathing a dog which is constantly trying to climb up the side of the bath or wander from end to end is not an easy task. An efficient shower attachment is a virtual necessity and you should not put the plug in the bath, for you will want the water to flow away freely. Be sure to test the temperature of the water, which should be neither too hot nor too cold, before you take your dog into the bathroom and be sure that you have sufficient hot water in the tank so that the water does not begin to run cold by the time you get around to rinsing off the conditioner. Male dogs, by the way, seem to be very particular about the water temperature on their testicles, so take especial care in this region. The bathroom should be pleasantly warm so that your dog does not get chilled when it comes out of the bath. If your dog is bathed regularly you may not need to shampoo twice, once being sufficient for a reasonably clean dog. Wet the coat thoroughly before applying the shampoo and most importantly, never rub the shampoo into the coat, for you will only rub in more matts and tangles than you began with. Stroke the shampoo into the coat in the direction in which it lies and squeeze through with your hands. Be sure to rinse out very thoroughly for if there is any shampoo left in the coat it will cause the coat to lack sheen and in dark-coloured dogs it can give rise to the appearance of dandruff. Conditioner should be applied in the same way as the shampoo and left in the coat for a few moments, or as long as directed, before rinsing out thoroughly.

You will be able to squeeze out some of the moisture from the long coat while the dog is still in the bath and then wrap it in a large warm towel. Under no circumstances use a rubbing motion with the towel or you will again only end up creating more knots. Instead, you should pat out any excess moisture and then lie the dog down on its side on the grooming table. If you have purchased one of the especially designed canine hair-dryers you will have both hands free for grooming your dog, and this, I assure you, will be a tremendous asset. A good canine dryer will speed up the process considerably, but don't allow the air flow to be too hot, nor too close to the coat. Take good care of your dryer and never allow it to get clogged with hair which inevitably flies about during the drying process. When drying your dog you will need to follow the same general procedure as described earlier for general grooming. Many dogs, understandably, object to having hot air blown directly on to their heads, so leave the head until last so that it has already dried slightly in the general warmth of the surrounding air. Never blow air directly on to the head and always protect eyes and nostrils with your free hand. Your dog should always be completely dried following a bath; do not be tempted to think that you can half-finish the dog and leave the rest until later. This would result in the dog getting cold, and its hair would tend to curl or even frizz. Should visitors arrive at bath-time I am afraid they will just have to be made to understand that you are busy! The sight of a freshly bathed Shih Tzu is well worth the effort you will have put in, and you will be surprised how visibly proud your Shih Tzu feels too.

KEEPING A SHIH TZU IN SHORT COAT

If you wish to keep your Shih Tzu in short coat, usually referred to as 'puppy trim', unless you are experienced with a pair of clippers, you would probably be best advised to take him to a professional grooming parlour three or perhaps four times a year. You can, of course, scissor the coat down yourself and a lot will depend on how talented you are with a pair of scissors and how good a finish on the coat you are prepared to accept. Some people, myself included, trim some dogs into a puppy trim just twice a year, at the close of summer, before the weather gets too cold, and again in the spring ready for the onset of summer. However, you should avoid suddenly clipping the coat short when the weather is very cold for this will be too much of a shock to the system. If, for some reason, you do have to clip down when the weather is colder than desirable, make sure that your Shih Tzu has plenty of extra bedding and, if it is kennelled outside it should have some form of heat in the kennel.

Keeping a Shih Tzu in short coat does not mean that you eliminate the need for frequent grooming sessions, merely that these will take less time. The undercoat will still grow in and matts can still form on a short coat, especially behind the ears. A daily check over and a weekly groom-out should still be maintained to keep your short-coated pet looking and feeling its best.

DAILY UP-KEEP

Finally, let us just quickly run down the list of things you will need to check on a daily basis for, in this way, you can be sure that your Shih Tzu will always be clean and comfortable and when you give a thorough grooming session you will subject neither your dog nor yourself to what could turn out to be an exceptionally long, sometimes uncomfortable, session.

1. After exercise always check the coat for any small pieces of debris which may have collected. If there is any sign of dirt on the feet give a quick check under the pads to see that nothing has become lodged.
2. Always keep a dry towel handy to use if your dog comes in with damp feet, but don't rub.
3. If your dog gets wet, dry it off thoroughly.
4. At any sign of scratching check cleanliness of ears and also for stray parasites – keep a tin of flea-spray in the cupboard for emergencies even if, hopefully, you never have to use it!
5. Check eyes on a daily basis and see that no discharge is allowed to remain.
6. Keep a careful eye on whiskers and beard to see that neither get sticky from food. Comb through daily.
7. Put head furnishings into a top-knot at least once each day, and remember always to cut out the elastic – never pull.
8. Check back of trousers and penis area to see that no soiling needs to be removed.

Chapter Eight

SHOW TRAINING
AND SHOWS

If you have purchased a puppy with a view to entering it in competition in the show ring you will, hopefully, have been giving it a little show training in your own home. This will usually reap rewards, for your puppy will already be comfortable standing on a table and will be used to walking on a lead. Practice walking with the lead in your left hand and, when you feel confident that you will not confuse the puppy by changing sides, walk it also on your right, for there will be times in the show ring when this is necessary so that you do not mask the judge's view of your exhibit with your own body. You will have trained your youngster to lie on its side to be groomed so that you allow yourself every opportunity of presenting its coat to perfection, something which is a necessity when exhibiting any of the long-coated breeds against the strong competition to be found in the rings today.

Some people take their youngsters to ringcraft (show training) classes when they are fully covered by the vaccination programme, and this can be a good way of socializing your Shih Tzu both with other dogs and with humans. I feel, however, that I must stress that you should be highly selective about the ringcraft class you choose, for though many are extremely good, there are some which are not. Your aim at this stage of the game is to learn as much as possible about the craft of showmanship and to do so you will need to be guided by those who already have a great deal of experience. Not all breeds are shown in the same way, and it goes without saying that you will, in most cases, be able to learn more from someone who is familiar with showing one of the small, long-coated breeds than from someone who has one of the large, long-legged breeds. The methods of show training are, in many respects, far removed from each other.

Ask others in your breed whether they can recommend a good training class within reasonably easy travelling distance of your home, and, unless you live in the depths of the countryside, as I do, you will usually find that there is a good one not too far away. If you have any difficulty in locating one, your local vet may be able to point you in the right direction, or the Kennel Club keeps a list of approved ringcraft societies. I would suggest that on the first visit you go along without your dog, just to see what is going on and to be sure that you feel sufficiently confident that those running the class are suitably conversant with small dogs. As an alternative, you may take your dog along just to watch that first night, for this will allow it to get used to the medley of strange sounds and all the different dogs, of varying sizes, which make up the class. When you do take your dog into a class, to begin with at least, try to stand next to dogs of similar size so that your dog does not feel over-powered, and always avoid landing yourself next to someone with an aggressive dog or one which the owner is unable to control.

When setting up your dog on the table, which is where the judge will examine each of the smaller dogs, teach it to stand still but never use force of any kind. Do not extend any limbs excessively and practice, in front of a mirror, creating a well balanced overall picture. Your Shih Tzu is sure to look more attractive if its head is held reasonably high, though not pointing skyward (often an indication of poor shoulder placement), and its tail should be presented over its back with the fringing draped to the side from which it is being viewed. Alternatively, the fringing can be divided neatly so that it hangs on both sides of the body, though this method of presentation is less common nowadays and only works well when the dog has fully mature tail furnishings. It may be that until your puppy has gained complete confidence in the ring you will need to encourage it to keep its tail up. This can be done by holding the tail over with your left hand, making sure your hand is as invisible as possible so that it does not detract from the overall picture. It is far better to hold the tail up than allow it to drop. In the majority of cases, you will find that as soon as your Shih Tzu begins to enjoy being in the show ring its tail will come up of its own accord.

You will also need to learn to move your dog at the pace which shows its movement off to best advantage. If you can get an experienced friend to watch you move your dog, and then give an honest opinion as to how quickly or slowly you should move, this will be a great help. Often puppies' fronts take time to strengthen and even a well constructed youngster can throw its legs when on the move, if you have not accurately assessed the best pace. You will also have to teach it not to pull on the lead, another bad habit which can play havoc with movement, even though the overall construction may be reasonably sound. Of course, if your Shih Tzu does have faulty construction this will almost certainly show up in its movement so you will have to learn to minimize its evidence by the pace at which you move. Having said that, whatever pace you do decide to move your exhibit, some judges will inevitably ask you to move again a little more quickly or more slowly so that they can more accurately assess the movement!

Provided that your Shih Tzu has been correctly registered with the Kennel Club it will be eligible for entry in shows from the age of six months. This means that you will have had to start thinking about shows well before then for, dependent upon the type of show, entries can close several weeks beforehand. Exemption Shows can be entered on the day, but these are really just for fun; the proceeds go to a charity, and there are never any specific breed classes on offer. Other shows, for which you must book in advance, include: Sanction, Limited, Open and Championship Shows, and if you plan to be a serious exhibitor you will most probably find that your concern is principally with the last two. If you are completely new to showing you would probably be wisest to start by entering a few Open Shows. These can usually be selected without the need to travel too great a distance, entry fees are not too expensive, the atmosphere is usually quite relaxed and competition is not generally so strong as at a Championship event. This means that you are more likely to get placed with your exhibit – always more rewarding than having to

This well-trained four and a half month old puppy is Bellakerne Scooby Do.

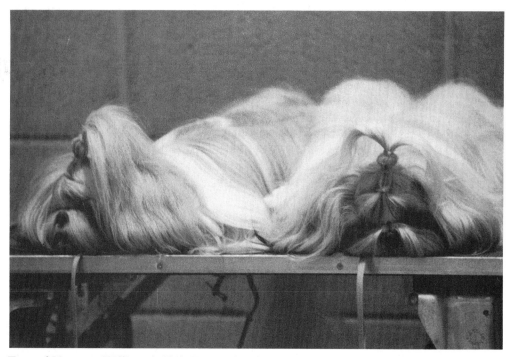

Two of Vanessa Williams' Shih Tzu make themselves comfortable while waiting to go into the ring.   *Photo by Carol Ann Johnson.*

leave the ring without a card. The number of dogs exhibited in a class varies greatly from show to show, depending on the time of year, day of the week, venue and, not least, the judge. At an Open Show there may be only three or four exhibits in your class whereas at a Championship Show you frequently find twenty or more. But that is not to say that some good dogs are not entered at Open Shows; they are, and it is always hard to get past an outstanding exhibit, whatever the show!

As Championship Shows are mostly benched (meaning that benches are provided on which dogs wait between classes), the entry fee is now around £11 per dog for entry in the first class with a lower fee for second and subsequent classes. By the time you have added the cost of car parking, catalogue, petrol and out of pocket expenses you can see that the financial layout for serious showing amounts to quite a hefty sum, especially if you are campaigning more than one dog. Entry costs at breed club shows are usually rather less; such Open and Championship shows held exclusively for Shih Tzu provide an excellent opportunity for meeting like-minded people. There are five Shih Tzu breed clubs in the UK at present, so there are plenty of shows to choose from. Hopefully one of the first things you did when you purchased your Shih Tzu was join one or more of the breed clubs and, if so, you will find that details of club shows have automatically been mailed to you.

When you have obtained your show schedule from the society's secretary, details having been published in the canine press, consider carefully which classes you should enter. Don't make the mistake, made by so many novices, of entering in every available class. The Open class, for instance, is open to all, but that can and frequently does include Champions and other top winning stock – an unfair test for your unfinished youngster. If your dog is really new to showing you should restrict it to exhibition in the most appropriate age class and perhaps just one other, such as Maiden or Novice, where the competition is less strong. The schedule will include a list of the qualifications needed to enter each class, and you will need to keep a careful record of your dog's wins so that you never mistakenly enter it in a class for which it is not eligible. Entries are pre-paid, and so if you own a bitch there is always the chance that you enter a show, and she comes into season just beforehand. There is no rule to say you cannot enter, but the owner of a bitch in full season is unlikely to be popular with exhibitors who have taken male dogs along to the show. The bitch may also be a bit skittish at the time of her season due to a change in hormone balance, and you may well decide that, all things considered, it is best to leave her at home and forego the entry fees.

Always allow yourself plenty of time to travel to a show; you may need to stop to exercise your dogs on the way and you could meet with unexpected traffic delays or long queues into the showground's car park. Nothing is more frustrating than travelling a long distance to a show only to find that you have missed your class. It is also a good idea to pack the car the night before, not forgetting to fill up with petrol in case you leave before the garages are open, and to check the canine press for notification of any change of judging times, something that happens with increasing frequency in breeds which attract high entries. If you wish to keep your costs down you would be well advised to take along a packed lunch and flask of coffee, something which is essential if travelling in the depth of winter when there is a risk of being stranded in the snow on the way to or from a show. Never, of course, forget to keep an ample supply of fresh water in the the car for your dog.

Hopefully you will arrive at the show in good time so that you can sort out where your bench is situated and its proximity to the ring. At major shows you may also find that there is a special

LEFT: Head study of the charming puppy bitch, Janmayen Betsinda (Harropine the Lion in Winter – Snaefells Sweet Margaretta of Janmayen), owned by Mesdames Pickburn and Duke.
Photo by Carol Ann Johnson.

BELOW: Bellakerne Misty Do (Zuthis Moonwalker – Ch. Bellakerne Pagan Do). This well presented young bitch, still only a puppy in this photo, has already learned the art of showmanship.
Photo by Carol Ann Johnson.

grooming area set aside for your breed and perhaps others which are being shown in adjacent rings. With a Shih Tzu you will need quite a lot of equipment, most of which has already been discussed in the previous chapter. If you need to buy any item, you will find that there are numerous stalls selling everything imaginable at the all-breed Championship shows. New exhibitors will need a ring-clip, something which you can buy for just a few pence at many of the stalls, and this is required to keep your ring number in place, for it must be clearly visible at all times. At a benched show ring numbers are usually to be found on your bench, but they may be given out by the steward in the ring or, at smaller shows, may be obtained from the Secretary's office. Make sure you know the whereabouts of your number before you go into the ring, for you want to be able to concentrate a hundred per cent on your dog, and the last thing you should be worrying about is your number.

An important rule for successful exhibitors is to keep your eye on the judge at all times, and that means from the very moment you enter the ring with your dog. Even though the judge may be enjoying a cup of coffee between classes you will notice that her eye may well wander along the line of dogs as they come into the class, so if you are not sure that your Shih Tzu will walk into the ring proudly and with confidence, carry it in so that the first opportunity the judge gets to see your dog is when it is stacked and presented for the judge's attention. Avoid standing next to someone who is renowned to be a chatterbox, for you will need to concentrate entirely on your exhibit, always keeping one eye on the judge so that you never miss an opportunity which may be given to you to move your dog again for further appraisal. Watch especially carefully when the judge is calling the winners into the centre of the ring, for if you do not go out when called, you may just find that you are not given a second chance.

Finally, whether you win or lose, do it with good grace. There is always another show and another judge and, who knows, the placings may be reversed next time around. It is usual, if your dog has been placed second or third, to congratulate the winner of the class and never under any circumstances should you refuse a prize card or rosette – that is the epitome of bad form and does, I am sorry to say, happen from time to time, risking grave consequences if the judge chooses to report this behaviour to the Kennel Club. If you don't agree with the judge's selection that is your prerogative, but you would be wise not to comment out loud. Remember that with a long coated breed such as the Shih Tzu, the judge is the only person who has had the opportunity to see what that glorious coat is concealing. Often a dog can be made to look especially good from the ringside, but its abundant coat covers a multitude of sins!

If you are lucky enough to win your class, of course you will be delighted, but do try not to boast too much about it. There are those who do so excessively, and they are never the most popular people among the dog-showing fraternity! If your dog has won a breed class, provided that it has not been beaten in another class, it will be eligible to compete for Best of Sex or Best of Breed, depending on the classification at the show. Under no circumstances withdraw it from such competition (unless, for example, the dog has gone lame), for this is also considered the height of bad manners. Likewise, if your dog is eligible to compete for Best in Group, Best in Show, or Best Puppy in Show, it is considered courteous to the judge who gave your exhibit that opportunity, to enter it for competition. If you are fortunate enough to have a major win, you should consider carefully whether to spend a little money advertising this win in the canine press. You will often find that there is an official photographer at the show and so you will be able to have a photograph taken for inclusion in your advertisement. Such advertising will bring attention to your dog's success, and it is always relevant to bear in mind that many of those who

At the LKA Championship Show in December 1991 judge Mrs Valerie Goodwin assesses the bitch class winners before awarding the Challenge Certificate. Left to right: Ch. Bowchild Promises Promises, Hot Favourite at Huxlor, Bellakerne Misty Do, Bellakerne Liza Do and Mandy's Christmas Cracker at Treeco.   *Photo by Carol Ann Johnson.*

read the canine press are not only exhibitors but also judges!

Looking on the negative side, if your "potential show dog" turns out not to be all you had hoped for in terms of its success in the show ring, love the dog for what it is and keep it as a much valued pet. After all, it is not the dog's fault that its legs grew a bit too long or its head went wrong as it out-grew puppyhood. Maybe you will decide to look for a Shih Tzu companion for it, and, thanks to your involvement through your first dog, you will have a better idea of what you are looking for next time.

Chapter Nine

MATING AND AFTERCARE

For the good of the breed it is essential that I open this chapter by stressing that you must give the subject of whether or not you should bring another litter into the world the most careful consideration. Once the mating has taken place it is too late!

SUITABILITY OF THE BITCH
Firstly, if you have a bitch you must be absolutely certain that she is of good enough quality to be used for breeding. It is all too easy to be 'kennel blind' and to overlook the magnitude of a bitch's faults, merely because you are obsessed by the desire to have a litter out of her, possibly with the aim of producing something a little bit better. My personal advice is that a bitch should only be bred from if she is good enough quality to be exhibited at Championship Show level and has had at least some measure of success. Breeding from poor quality stock makes for a long hard climb if you are ever to produce anything which is truly typical of the breed, and faults can take many generations to breed out, sometimes raising their ugly heads when you least expect it. So, whether or not you show your Shih Tzu bitch, if you are seriously considering allowing her to have a litter, take expert advice on whether or not she is of sufficient merit. By expert advice, I do not only mean discussing the matter with your vet, you also need to talk to a couple of judges, preferably at Championship level in the breed, for they will have had the opportunity to go over many high quality specimens, and they are therefore in the best possible position to compare the merits of your own bitch against others.

Given that you are completely satisfied that you have a true representative of the breed, sound both in body and in mind, dismiss entirely any comments that you may have heard about it being good for a bitch to have a litter, or that by having a litter she will no longer have false pregnancies or is less likely to get pyometra. Such statements are invariably made by those who wish them to be true, but they are not founded on fact. The reason that you want a litter should

This striking black and white litter is by Tricina Chi-Fu – Whitethroat Chi-Wu to Delridge, the result of a half-brother/sister mating.   *Photo courtesy Eileen Wilson.*

be that you feel your bitch is so good that you would like her to procreate, and hopefully it will be your plan to keep one of her puppies so that you can, in later years, develop your own line. You must also be absolutely certain that you have both the time and the finances available to bring up a litter. A first litter especially can be quite a costly affair, with a stud fee to find, equipment to buy, vet's bills to pay, a hungry bitch to feed and rapidly growing puppies, who need to be kept warm and be fed on high quality food. You cannot hold down a full-time job and successfully raise a litter of puppies, and even if you only work part-time you will need to arrange time off for a few days around the time that the litter is due, bearing in mind that your bitch may whelp early or late. Although you may wish to keep one of the puppies yourself, you need to ensure that you have sufficient suitable, permanent homes available for the rest of the litter, and you will need to vet buyers with extreme care to be as sure as you can that your carefully reared puppies do not fall into the wrong hands. And if, by chance, one or more of your intending purchasers falls by the wayside, you must be able to keep any unsold puppies as long as necessary until the right homes are found. Looking still further ahead, should unforeseen circumstances prevent someone from keeping the Shih Tzu which they have bought from you, it is your duty as a reputable breeder either to have the dog back or to play a constructive part in re-settling the dog in a new home. There is more to breeding a litter of puppies than first meets the eye.

STUD DOGS

Before we move on to the mating itself, it would be prudent to look at the subject of the stud dog. First and foremost, no pet dog should ever be used at stud. There are sufficient high quality stud dogs whose services are available for there never to be a need to use a pet dog who is purely a family companion, however good he may be. A dog is usually used at stud far more times than a bitch has litters, and if you have a pet dog you may well only find one person wishing to use him, and that will probably be an inexperienced 'breeder' who is merely using him for the sake of convenience. Once a dog has been used at stud, his desire to mate will almost certainly be strengthened and you may well find that a family pet who was once perfectly clean around the house, starts to leave scent marks in every available corner. He may also become much more possessive so that you see an outward change in his temperament. A young dog who gets over-excited and tries to mate human legs, to the embarrassment of his owners, will not necessarily be cured by experiencing the real thing. Clearly an over-sexed dog is not easy to live with and reprimand does not always work, though usually this is simply one of the stages of growing up and within a few months, provided the dog has not been used at stud, he will grow out of it. If this is not the case, castration may be the answer, and the subject should be discussed with your vet.

STUD FEES
For those dogs which are used at stud, a fee will usually be charged for the service, or there may be an arrangement whereby the owner of the dog has a puppy back in lieu of a stud fee. Naturally, any agreement reached must be clearly set down in writing so that both parties concerned know exactly what was decided and exactly what is to be done if the mating does not result in the intended litter of puppies, or if only one puppy is whelped, for the breeder would probably be very reluctant to let a singleton puppy go to the stud dog owner. If a fee is paid, this is for the service and not for the litter produced, so that unless it has been agreed otherwise, the fee is paid immediately after the first mating and is not refundable. Most stud dog owners allow the dog to mate the bitch twice, usually with one day in between, and if the bitch does not have live puppies another mating is usually made available at no extra charge at the bitch's subsequent season. But I stress that this must all be agreed from the outset. A practice which is rapidly disappearing is that if a stud dog is unproven a free service is given to the first bitch he mates, and it is, of course, preferable if his very first bitch is already experienced so that at least one of the pair knows what to do! Some stud dogs seem proficient from the outset but others do the most peculiar things at their first attempt, so that experienced handlers and an experienced bitch are invaluable assets. It is certainly not wise to allow a dog to mate a bitch below the age of ten months and, subsequent to his first mating, it is usually thought advisable to give him a couple of months' rest before he mates his second bitch.

SELECTION OF A STUD
Your aim should always be to improve on your current stock and to do that you must, of necessity, select the stud dog with the very greatest of care. If this is to be your first litter you should seek the advice of those more experienced than yourself, but do not be misled into using someone's stud dog against your better judgement. You will need to select a dog which is compatible with your bitch, and this is generally done by studying various pedigrees to see how they will match up with the bitch concerned. You will also need to look at the prospective stud dogs, and at what they have produced – some of their progeny will hopefully be available for you to see in the show-ring. The subject is a complex one, and I would most strongly suggest

that you read as much as you can about the various types of breeding (in-breeding, line-breeding and out-crossing) for the subject in its entirety cannot be covered within the confines of a breed book. For your first mating you would most probably be wise to line-breed, looking very carefully at both the positive and negative aspects of the dogs which feature most in the pedigree.

Strictly speaking, geographical location should not play an important part in the selection of a sire, and under no circumstances should you merely choose the stud dog which happens to live the closest to your home or, for that matter, the one which is currently doing the greatest amount of winning. Of course, there is just a chance that one of these might really be the most suitable dog for your particular bitch, but if an inconveniently located stud or a lesser known dog is the one you truly feel is right, then you should not allow either convenience or prestige to alter your judgement. Do be sure to give the stud dog owner plenty of warning as to when your bitch is likely to come into season, for the dog may be booked to other bitches and it may well be that his owner prefers to restrict the frequency of his use at stud. You should also have another dog lined up, just in case the dog of your choice decides to have nothing to do with your bitch. Dogs, regrettably, can sometimes be highly selective in their choice of mate as, indeed, can bitches. Be thoroughly honest with the owner of the reserve dog, making it clear that you only wish to use his dog if the first planned mating is not a success. If you are lucky your second choice might be owned by the same person, possibly a son of your preferred choice, for example.

THE TIME OF MATING

Firstly, it is essential that your bitch is not allowed to produce a litter of puppies until she is at least eighteen months of age, and most breeders like their bitches to have had their first litter by the time they are four years old. Depending on how frequently your bitch comes into season (for not all of them come in like clockwork at six monthly intervals), you will probably be planning a first mating at her third or fourth season. You will need to keep a very careful check on your bitch so that there is no risk of missing the beginning of her season and, although you will have already booked the stud dog you will need to alert his owner at the first sign of your bitch's season.

Most bitches are only receptive to the male for a few days of the season, frequently this spans about four days around the twelfth to sixteenth day but lines and individual bitches differ, and it has been known for some bitches to be receptive at the very beginning of the period of heat and others at the very end. There are also those who will only accept a male for a couple of days, so you can see that timing plays a very important part in achieving a successful mating. You may well find that the stud dog owner is willing to keep your bitch for a few days to facilitate the situation, but do be prepared to pay for your bitch's board if this is requested. The sign that a bitch is receptive is a softening of the vulva, so feel it carefully when she is not in season, placing your thumb horizontally across the uppermost part, in this way you will be more easily aware of the changes. As she comes into season the vulva will soften and enlarge and when she is ready for mating it will be at its softest; at this time she will most probably readily flick her tail to one side when you touch her nether regions. Readiness for mating is often also indicated by a lessening of the loss of colour, but this is not true for every bitch so don't count on this as a guide.

It goes without saying that your bitch must be in tip-top condition if she is to be mated, and you should not be dismayed if a stud dog owner asks you to have your bitch swabbed by the vet to prove that she is clear of infection which could be passed on to the dog. Indeed, a swab is never a bad idea for if your bitch does have an infection at the time of mating, you can have all sorts of problems with the resultant litter.

THE MATING

The bitch should always visit the dog, and under no circumstances should you arrange to meet the stud dog at a halfway point so that the mating can take place in some secluded spot – however suitable or unsuitable it may appear to be! If you have planned for your bitch to stay with the owner of the stud dog you will need to take along her own blanket or basket so that you give her every opportunity of feeling as much at home as possible in a strange environment. Naturally, many owners are reluctant to be parted from their bitches and in ideal circumstances I believe it is preferable for the owners to take the bitch along simply for the mating. However, most young ladies settle down extremely well if left for a short while, although some are reluctant to eat as well as they would at home.

When you go along for the mating please do not go along armed with your entire family, a mating is not a biology lesson for the children, and neither your host nor the stud dog will take kindly to a whole crowd of people in attendance. You should have a suitably strong leather collar for your bitch, for however docile she may be there is always a chance that when being mated she will turn to snap at whatever is nearest, especially if she is a maiden bitch, for she will be taken entirely by surprise at the penetration of the male. A mating usually needs two people to assist, one to take control of the bitch and one the dog. It may well be that the stud dog's owner already has an experienced person to assist with the mating but, if not, your help may be required, in which case you must be prepared to be very firm and not to panic.

Once the dog has penetrated there will be a 'tie', meaning that dog and bitch are locked together for a while (anything from a few minutes to an hour or more), the dog's penis having swollen and the bitch's vulva contracted. Many dogs wish to turn shortly following ejaculation, but they must never be forced to do so. Actually some of them perform the most astounding contortions, ending up back to back or even lying down, but still, of course, tied. Do be sure that a fresh drink of water is available at arm's length, so that they may have refreshment if they wish, though most will decline for they are far too involved in what is going on. As the muscles loosen off, the dog will start to fidget about and you will soon realize that he has released himself from the bitch. The stud dog owner must check to see that the penis has returned to its sheath for, especially with long coated breeds, the hair may have got caught up, preventing its immediate retraction, but this can usually be rectified with ease. Personally, I always like my dogs and bitches to remain in each other's company for a little while afterwards for they usually settle down quietly to relax. However, do not take your eyes off them for you do not wish your bitch to relieve herself for at least half an hour or so following the mating. Usually it is at this time that the financial side of the agreement is settled and a signed copy of the prospective sire's pedigree is officially handed over.

SLIP MATINGS

Slip matings are an extreme nuisance, for one can never be entirely sure whether the mating has been successful. A slip mating is when the dog penetrates and ejaculates but no tie takes place, and sometimes it is not clear whether or not any of his sperm has actually ended up inside the bitch. This can sometimes happen with an inexperienced stud or one who is rather too enthusiastic about the job in hand. Although I have known cases of puppies being produced as a result of a slip mating, I would always strongly recommend that a second mating is given. It may be that this can be left to the next day or, if the dog is not unduly tired it may be possible to have a break for lunch or dinner and try again a few hours later. A lot will depend, of course, on the set of circumstances and the time of day.

POINTS TO BEAR IN MIND

There are some breeders who like a bitch to be mated three times during her season but, personally, I feel that twice should be quite sufficient except perhaps if one of the matings was slipped and unlikely to have been successful. However many matings are given they should not span a period of too many days, for puppies can be conceived at each mating and those resulting from the first mating will be more developed than the later ones at the time of whelping. This can sometimes lead to problems at whelping time and can result in a rather uneven litter.

Always be very careful that no other dog mates your bitch while she is in season, for she could produce puppies by both sires and this will lead to obvious confusion when the puppies are born, and complications will of course arise when attempting to register them with the Kennel Club.

THE PREGNANCY

Many bitches show almost immediate signs of being in whelp, but to the untrained eye such signs are not always readily recognisable and, in any event, they cannot be counted upon. A slight enlargement of the bitch's nipples can often be seen and they are frequently rather more pink in colour than is normal. It is also likely that her vulva will not quite shrink down to its original size. Whatever you do, do not poke around in her abdomen to see what you can or cannot feel. Time will tell, and growth of the puppies within the first few weeks of pregnancy is extremely slow, so that she will be four or five weeks in whelp by the time you begin to see any noticeable change in her size. Even then, some bitches carry their whelps high up in the abdomen making it even more difficult to assess the situation. By the fifth week the mammary glands will have developed more fully and around the seventh week they will become rather soft. Milk will be usually found in the teats some little while before the puppies are actually born.

You should make no attempt to over-feed your bitch from the minute she has been mated, for all you will do is create an over-weight bitch. By the sixth week in whelp her food intake should have gradually increased by about a third, but she will require her food little and often, split into three or four small meals a day. I believe there is no reason to pump her full of supplements, but good proprietary multi-vitamin tablets, given exactly as per the directions, will be of benefit both while she is in whelp and when she is feeding her puppies. Some breeders like to give calcium, either in liquid or tablet form, before the bitch whelps, but I now prefer only to administer calcium (in liquid) from the day of whelping. If you are in any doubt about the merits of this, it would be wise to consult your vet.

Although your bitch should not be allowed to over exert herself and must certainly be prevented from jumping on and off furniture and such-like, moderate regular exercise should be encouraged so that she keeps her muscle tone. She must, however, be allowed to rest as frequently as she wishes and after the fourth week in whelp she should not be allowed in the company of other particularly exuberant dogs, unless under strict supervision. You should always use extreme care when lifting your pregnant bitch, especially when she is heavily in whelp, making sure that her body weight is fully supported at all times. Your bitch will probably have a tendency to rely on you more than normal as her pregnancy develops, but do not be tempted to over-fuss her, just give her the reassurance she needs. About ten days before she is due to whelp she should be introduced to her whelping box, which should be located completely out of draughts and in a quiet corner of the house where neither she nor her puppies, when they arrive, will be unduly disturbed at rest times. Although she may be reluctant to use her whelping box at first she must be encouraged to do so in order that she feels thoroughly at home there when whelping time comes around. All the time she has been pregnant you should have kept her coat in good condition, whether or not you have decided to keep it long or short. In the last few days of her pregnancy and for a few days after the litter is born she will have no desire to be subjected to lengthy grooming sessions. You will probably find the hair around the teats has gone rather sparse of its own accord, but two or three days before you expect her to whelp you should carefully trim the coat in this area so that it does not impede the puppies in any way when they are suckling. I also like to trim long coated bitches around their back-end in order that they stay as clean and dry as is possible during the whelping and while there is a mucus discharge for a few days afterwards.

A whelping chart will help you to determine the date when puppies can be expected, but although the normal gestation period is sixty-three days, three days either side of that date is perfectly normal. Indeed, I have frequently heard of puppies being born a week early or even a week late without ill effect. Having said that, if your bitch has not whelped within three days of the due date it would be wise to take her along to the vet to be checked. I always like to advise my vet about a week before a litter is due so that he is not taken by surprise if I have to call him in the middle of the night to ask his advice because of a whelping problem. In my experience most bitches seem to whelp in the small hours, and so a good rapport with your vet is an essential part of successful breeding.

EQUIPMENT FOR WHELPING

WHELPING BOX: You may choose to buy a ready constructed whelping box, but most breeders make one of their own. For a Shih Tzu, a box about 90cm x 75cm (3ft x 2ft 6ins) is sufficient, though an extra few inches in either direction would also be alright. Basically your bitch will need to feel cosy and comfortable, and she may like to push her back legs against the side of the box as she whelps. I always like to have a flap at the front so that I can lower this completely during the whelping process. It is very useful if this front flap can be fitted with two heights when erect: it can be quite low while the puppies are tiny so that Mum can see what is going on around her while she is still spending much of her time in the box, and as the puppies grow, both in stature and in liveliness, and as their dam chooses to spend more of her time away from the litter, the higher flap can be added to keep all the youngsters safely contained. Never underestimate their gymnastic prowess! I like to have a detachable run also made to fit the front of the box so that for certain periods each day, such as at feeding time, I can lower the flap and the youngsters can have more room to exercise while still being entirely out of harm's way.

It is essential that the whelping box itself is fitted with a guard rail to prevent the bitch from squashing any of her puppies against the side of the box. Unfortunately accidents do sometimes occur, and a guard rail is one of the most helpful ways of preventing this. The rail should be approximately 75mm (3 inches) from the floor of the box and should extend outward by about the same distance. Ideally, it should be removable so that when the puppies are up and about and there is no longer any danger of the bitch sitting on them, the rail can be removed, making a little more space in the box. The box should be thickly lined with clean newspaper, and I like to have this covered with a piece of veterinary bedding which gives warmth and allows moisture to soak through so that it does not remain on the surface of the bedding.

HEAT LAMP: Some people use heat pads but I prefer a heat lamp, suspended about 100cm (40 inches) above the base of the box. It should be entirely safe (some come fitted with a protective cage below the lamp) and needs to be adjustable in height so that it can be raised slightly as the puppies grow. It should also be located slightly off-centre so that both bitch and puppies can be out of direct heat should they prefer. Some lamps give off light and others heat only. If like me, you select the latter, I would strongly suggest that a dim light is left on in the room at all times while the puppies are tiny so that the bitch can see exactly what she is doing and, most importantly, what she is treading on!

KITCHEN TOWELLING: Make sure you have half a dozen rolls of pure white kitchen towelling available for the whelping. It is useful for a multitude of things such as keeping the bitch as clean as possible and rubbing down the puppies as they are whelped.

WATER: If there is a sink in the whelping room this is ideal. If not, a bowl of water must be available at all times. Naturally, you must also have a bowl of water, preferably containing a little glucose, available for your bitch but this must be well out of the way of the puppies in case of accident.

NAIL BRUSH AND SURGICAL SCRUB: During the whelping and while the puppies are very young, it is essential that your hands and nails are thoroughly clean to avoid introducing infection.

CARDBOARD BOXES: One box, containing a hot-water bottle, and lined with veterinary bedding will be needed for the whelps when they have been born. Do not take them away from the bitch any more frequently than necessary, but I find it easier for the whelps to be in a warm, safe place as each new whelp arrives, and usually the bitch is perfectly happy with this arrangement. The puppies should be covered with a clean white towel, for this settles them and tends to keep them quiet so as not to disturb the bitch. A second box, outside the door of the whelping room, can be used in the unfortunate event of there being any dead or malformed puppies.

KITCHEN SCALES: Some people do not like to weigh the puppies as they are born, but I always do and, provided that it is done quickly and discretely, I find that it does not disturb the bitch. The scales should be as deep as possible and lined with kitchen towelling, and I find it easiest and safest for them to be on the floor immediately next to the whelping box. My own preference is to weigh the puppies every day for the first couple of weeks, for this makes you immediately aware of any loss of weight indicating that something might be wrong. After the first two weeks, and providing that all seems well, I weigh on a weekly basis.

CLOCK, NOTEBOOK & PENCIL: You will need to keep an accurate record not only of the weight of each whelp but also the time at which each puppy is born, so that you are aware of any excessive delay between the delivery of each whelp. It is also wise to make a note of the first major push before delivery begins. If there is an excessive delay, a call to your vet would be a wise precaution, for it could indicate that a puppy is trapped in the birth canal.

SCISSORS: These should be sharp but blunt-ended and must be sterilized ready for use should you need to cut the umbilical cord.

STERILIZING TABLETS: Everything used during the whelping process must have been sterilized, and the most convenient method of sterilization is the use of tablets.

MILD DISINFECTANT: Any disinfectant used must be mild and of the type suitable for cleansing wounds.

PLASTIC SACKS AND/OR BUCKETS: It is essential that the whelping room should be kept spotlessly clean and tidy, despite the fact that there is a seemingly ever increasing mountain of soiled newspaper and kitchen towelling. Suitable plastic disposable sacks or buckets with tight-fitting lids are therefore a necessity.

PREMATURE BABY BOTTLE: You will need to have a bottle available in case you need to hand-rear one or more of the whelps. Make sure that the bottle is acquired before the litter is born, for they are not always readily available. Personally I find that a premature baby bottle is much easier to use than a cat-feeding bottle. It can be obtained through a chemist, vet, GP or hospital. Make sure that you get several spare teats.

GLUCOSE: Glucose in powdered form (available from any chemist) will be useful to give added nourishment to the bitch and is sometimes required if a young whelp needs to be hand-fed but is too young to take a milk substitute.

MILK SUBSTITUTE: A good quality proprietary milk substitute for puppies should be at hand in case it is needed either for complete hand-rearing or for supplementary feeding.

Chapter Ten

WHELPING AND WEANING

I cannot stress enough that if you have not whelped a litter before, or even if you have done so but not for a long while, you should read as much as you possibly can on the subject by the time your bitch is ready to whelp. Also make sure that a clear, comprehensive book is on hand in the whelping room, for in the panic of the moment it is only too easy to forget whether the book said such and such, or something completely different. I don't for one minute suggest that you will spend all your time in the whelping room reading a book, you will have far more urgent things to do, I just caution you to have immediate access to information should it be needed.

APPROACHING WHELPING DAY
Some people like to take a bitch's temperature leading up to the day of whelping, but this is not something which everyone feels comfortable doing, and the last thing you want to do is upset your bitch. I would therefore suggest that you only use a thermometer for guidance if you have had expert tuition as to how to use it. Those who use this method generally take the temperature for the first time on the fifty-seventh day when it should be somewhere between 100 degrees and 101.4 degrees fahrenheit. By the sixty-first day a second reading will need to be taken so that the drop in temperature can be registered immediately it begins. At this point shivering commences but the temperature will then suddenly rise again, possibly to as much as 102 degrees. This is the point at which the bitch usually begins to start pushing.

It is equally important to note the outward signs of a bitch going into labour, as bitches do not always whelp on the due date, some come early, and many an unfortunate accident has occurred because the bitch's owner did not keep a careful enough eye on her charge about a week before the whelping was expected. Your bitch will probably refuse food at least a few hours and possibly as long as a full day before she begins to whelp. This is quite normal. She may also vomit slightly. Provided that it is not excessive and seems not to be causing any discomfort, this is no cause for concern. For the last few days she may have been nest-making in a half-hearted manner, but as the day and hour approaches she will work vigorously at her task. She should by now be thoroughly familiar with her whelping box, and an experienced bitch will probably seek it out, for she knows full well that her time is approaching.

When a bitch has reached the nest-making stage she should be carefully supervised when out in the garden, for some bitches have a habit of trying to make a nest discretely under a bush, and you would never forgive yourself if your bitch was left alone long enough to start whelping outside, possibly in a temperature which would be far too cold for the young whelps. When you accompany your bitch outside make sure that the exercise area is fully lit or that you have a torch – one in good working order for batteries invariably start to fade at the wrong moment! The bitch's teats will most probably have begun to fill with milk, and she may appear restless, looking to you for comfort and following you around more than you would normally expect her to. It is highly likely that she will also be panting, though this can go on for several hours, if not a complete day or more. I used to whelp my bitches in my large, heated bathroom, and I well remember feeling certain that one of my ladies would whelp during the early hours of the morning, so settled down with her for what I expected to be just a couple of hours before action stations. I woke up the next morning to find my head trapped under the lavatory basin, and she didn't whelp until just turned midnight – the next day!

WHELPING

Not long before the bitch whelps, she will have started to shiver, frequently turning around to lick her vulva which will have softened and be producing a clear or whitish mucous discharge. If she is losing any deep colour at this stage your vet must be consulted at once. Sooner or later you will see her strain visibly, indicating that there is movement of the puppies along the birth canal. It is likely that during the last few days of her pregnancy you have been able to feel the puppies moving about in her abdomen, but this will usually have quietened down for the last couple of days before the second stage of labour begins. The time of her first major strain must be noted and you should find that the strains increase in frequency, probably starting off about every fifteen minutes or so, the intervals between them becoming less and less frequent until a bubble appears at the vaginal entrance, this probably following a gush of fluid as a prelude to the puppy being forced out of the vagina. The bubble will indicate that the puppy is still in its sac, a good sign, and hopefully, given one or two more strong pushes, she will have produced one live whelp encased in its sac. If she has not produced a puppy within about an hour and a half of the first strong push, your vet should be consulted, for this could perhaps indicate that there is something obstructing the passage of the first whelp. But, hopefully, all will be progressing smoothly and you now have one puppy in sac, followed by the placenta (afterbirth) to which it is attached.

You may find that your bitch instinctively knows just what to do and breaks both sac and umbilical cord herself. However, Shih Tzu, being one of the shorter-nosed breeds, often have some difficulty in carrying out this procedure and even when they do so run a slight risk of injuring the puppy, sometimes tugging so violently on the cord that they create a small umbilical hernia (in this instance caused through trauma as opposed to it being hereditary). A maiden bitch, producing her very first whelp, will probably be somewhat overcome and bemused by the situation, and for the safety of the puppy you will need to help her out. The sac containing the puppy will need to be broken at the end which contains the puppy's head. You will be able to tear this, but I have known whelps to be encased in a double sac making this quite surprisingly difficult. However, it is essential that the head is released so that the puppy is able to breathe and you will need to wipe clear the air passages to facilitate this.

I have known of cases when the puppy has been expelled but the placenta has been left inside the bitch for up to twenty minutes and, with the sac removed and the air passages clear, the puppies have suckled quite happily on one of the lower teats! However, given that both puppy and placenta are delivered together and the puppy has access to an air supply, the next step is to cut the umbilical cord, if the bitch has not done so. Firstly, pinch the cord, press the blood supply within it in the direction of the whelp and then either cut or tear (I prefer to do the latter) at least one inch away from the puppy's umbilicus. The use of sterilised thread tied around the cord will only be necessary in cases of excessive bleeding. If the placenta does not come away of its own accord never pull on it too heavily, for it may be still attached to the bitch and pulling could therefore cause a haemorrhage. Another reason for the placenta failing to come away shortly after the the puppy has been born is if it is trapped around another puppy, in which case it will probably be expelled with the next whelp.

It is instinctive for the bitch to wish to eat her placentas, and occasionally she will do so before you have time to take them away. I am perfectly happy to allow my bitches to eat two, or perhaps three, for they do provide nourishment, and I know that she will probably not fancy much in the way of real food for the next twenty-four hours. However, with a larger litter I do not think it wise to allow her to eat all of the placentas for this will make her motions loose, a problem which both she and you can do without while she is bringing up a litter of tiny puppies. The bitch will most probably be content to clean up each puppy as it is born and it is best to leave her, to a greater or lesser extent, to her own devices, provided that she does not appear to be handling the puppies too roughly – though it is surprising quite how much rough and tumble such tiny things can take from their dam! When she begins to push in earnest to produce the next puppy, you will usually find that she is quite willing to let you discretely take away her first-born puppies. It is now that they should be put into the cardboard box, based with a well-wrapped, not-too-hot, hot-water bottle. This will also probably provide you with an opportunity to quickly weigh the last whelp, and to jot down the sex and any distinctive markings. I also like to check at this stage for cleft palate, for I feel it kinder that the discovery is made at the earliest possible opportunity, for there will be little hope of success in rearing the youngster to maturity.

As soon as the bitch has produced her next puppy she will be anxious to have all the others back with her, so don't deprive her of their company for too long. Try to keep an eye on which puppies are suckling and which are not, for it is important that all receive the protective antibodies contained in the early milk supply. In ideal circumstances all previous whelps should have suckled by the time the last is born. If one or more seem to have difficulty in starting to suckle, your bitch will probably not be disturbed if you hold a poor sucker to a teat that has already been used, and, if necessary, squeezing a little of the milk on to the puppy's lips to give it the idea.

It will be appreciated that it is not possible to give intricate details of the various types of abnormal whelpings which might possibly occur, but the following information may be of some assistance:-

INERTIA: Inertia can occur in either the first or second stages of labour and, without going into great detail, it involves the bitch's lack of ability to produce her whelps. Primary inertia will preclude her from actually going into labour at all, possibly the result of a very small litter which does not generate sufficient hormone, or a large litter resulting in an over-stretched uterus which does not begin to contract. Secondary inertia occurs when she has started to whelp but then stops trying to expel the whelps, either because the uterus has stopped contracting or because she has simply tired herself out. If there is an exceedingly long delay between puppies your vet will need to be consulted and, if the problem cannot be solved by some other means, a caesarian operation will be performed to release the remaining whelps.

MALPRESENTATION OF A WHELP: Not all puppies are produced head-first, but those which are are the easiest ones for the bitch to expel. In Shih Tzu, as in other breeds, as many as forty per cent of the litter can present feet-first. Provided that the spine of the puppy is uppermost this is not a breach birth and rarely creates any problem. A breach is when the puppy is hind legs first and upside down, which is more difficult to expel. Occasionally a puppy will be presented sideways on and will need to be turned. Inexperienced breeders will certainly need to consult their vets in such circumstances but, for the more experienced, it may well be possible to turn the whelp to facilitate the birth. Under no circumstances should you pull at the whelp unless the bitch is pushing, so timing is of the utmost importance.

STILL-BORN PUPPIES: Occasionally, especially in cases where a puppy has spent too long in the vaginal tract, a puppy will be still born. Provided that you are confident that the puppy is otherwise 'perfectly' formed and that it has only recently expired through lack of oxygen you can certainly try to revive it, but you must act quickly, preferably somewhere out of sight of the bitch. Clear the airways as you would do normally, and rub its back and chest briskly with a rough, warm towel. If you are very lucky you will have instant success, but if not, take it firmly in both hands, one supporting the back of the head and the other the back and rear end and, with the puppy's head facing downwards and making sure that the tongue is well forward, swing it through the air, up and down, between your legs. If you still fail to meet with success, a drop of neat brandy on the tongue or, alternatively, the use of smelling salts, may just make the puppy gasp and thus begin to breathe. Although I have not ever had occasion to use the latter method I can see that it might well work, for I did once revive an apparently dead mouse with dry white wine! Some people suggest breathing into the puppy's mouth, but I do not advocate this method for it is difficult to ascertain how much air the puppy's lungs are capable of taking. If you find that the tongue is white, indicating that the puppy has been dead for a longer period, it would not be wise to attempt resuscitation, for prolonged lack of oxygen will have caused damage to the brain.

RETAINED PLACENTAS: It is important that you count the placentas expelled by the bitch for, whether or not you have allowed her to eat any of them, you will need to know that all have come away. If any have been retained this can set up infection. Should you be unsure whether or not all have been expelled you should discuss this with your vet who will probably give an injection to release any which may remain.

CAESAREAN SECTION

If things do not go smoothly, the ultimate decision as to whether or not a caesarian operation is carried out will rest with your vet. However, do not be afraid to discuss this with him in full so that you are completely aware of why it needs to be done and when. Vets' opinions do vary quite considerably as to how soon following the due date an operation needs to be performed. I know of those who are anxious to operate when a bitch is three days over-due, and others who are not unduly concerned if the puppies have still not arrived a week late. A lot depends on the circumstances and, of course, the condition of your bitch. The danger of losing your bitch during such an operation is relatively low these days, but any operation carries some element of risk, and the risk factor is increased if she is already exhausted from her attempts to produce the litter on her own. It must therefore not be taken lightly. The prime reasons for a caesarian operation are:-

Malpresentation: A puppy in a position which precludes it from passing normally through the birth canal. This can also block the way for subsequent puppies and can cause danger to the dam.

An exceptionally large puppy: The puppy is so large that the bitch is unable to expel it. This can sometimes be because it is a singleton (a litter of one).

Uterine inertia: This is a lack of visible contractions, even though other signs of the birth process are evident.

A long, exhausting labour: The bitch may have produced some, but not all of the puppies. As a result she will gradually have weakened so that uterine and abdominal contractions have ceased.

Abnormal pelvic aperture: This could be due to a previous pelvic fracture or to a construction of the hindquarters resulting in difficulty in passing puppies normally. If there is any doubt as to a bitch's suitability for breeding she should be checked over by a vet before a decision is taken to have her mated. In the case of a previous accident where there was injury to the pelvis, there is always a danger of internal trouble, even though there are no outward signs of damage.

When a caesarian operation has been performed, your bitch will hopefully be fully alert by the time she comes home. The puppies should not be returned to her until she is fully conscious, for when a bitch has not actually gone through the process of whelping (except in cases where she has produced one or more of the whelps herself) it may well take her longer than usual to accept the puppies. It is therefore a good idea to return them to her one at a time so that she is not totally confused by the entire litter. Try to get each puppy in turn to take some of her milk as the colostral antibodies will only be present in her milk supply for between twenty-four and forty-eight hours. She will need rather special care and you will need to keep an eye on her when she goes out to spend a penny in case she pops any of her stitches. Soon the bitch will treat her puppies as though she had had a normal delivery, and you will be surprised how she tolerates the kneading of the puppies' feet on her tender stomach. There are cases when a bitch which has had one caesarian operation is able whelp another litter quite normally, but if she were to need a second caesarian it would be most unwise to mate her again. If she has had a caesarian it is essential that you discuss the matter fully with your vet before you consider mating her on a subsequent occasion.

POST WHELPING

When the whelping is over the bitch will be reluctant to be parted from her new litter, but a short while after you are certain that the last puppy has been produced, take her outside to give her the opportunity to relieve herself, although she will almost certainly be reluctant to do so. Stay with her while she is outside (just in case there was another whelp tucked up in the rib-cage) and give her a very quick freshen up, especially around her back end, before she goes back to her puppies. Be sure that she is offered plenty of glucose water, but don't expect her to get out of the whelping box for at this stage she will most probably not want to leave her litter, even for a drink. Do not leave water in the box, for this is a potential danger to the young whelps. The bitch will not feel like eating yet, but I often find that my bitches are grateful for a whisked egg yolk (don't give the white), mixed with a little milk, and you can include the first dose of liquid calcium in this. The calcium can also be syringed into the bitch's mouth if the she does not wish to eat the egg.

The bitch should, by now, be content to settle down with her litter, but if she is still showing signs of distress you should most certainly contact your vet, for there is a chance that something is amiss, possibly retention of a dead puppy. In any event, especially if you are inexperienced, it would be wise to have your veterinary surgeon check the bitch to see that everything is in order. He may decide to give an injection of pituitrin and perhaps antibiotics to help expel any placentas which might possibly remain and to speed up the contraction of the uterus. Bear in mind, however, that your bitch will not wish to be away from her puppies for too long so it is probably worth the additional 'call out' fee to have your vet visit your home. If you have to go to the surgery, depending on its proximity, you will most probably need to take the puppies along as well. They should be transported in a secure cardboard box, with a wrapped hot-water bottle in the base and they should be lightly covered with a clean towel; this will prevent them from crying. Make sure the vet knows that you are on your way so that you do not have to wait too long in the waiting room – especially during surgery hours – and don't be afraid to ask the receptionist for a top-up in the hot-water bottle so that the puppies have an equally comfortable journey home. Obviously consultation with a vet at this stage will also give him the opportunity to check the puppies over to see that there is nothing wrong.

THE EARLY WEEKS

During the first couple of weeks the bitch will want to spend virtually all her time with the puppies, but that does not mean to say that she will not need to know that you are around in the background, ready to assist her should ever the need arise. Sometimes, for a example, a puppy may have strayed to a far corner of the box and she cannot retrieve it, being reluctant to leave the rest of the litter if feeding. The puppy must in such cases be replaced on a teat, for it will weaken and fail to survive if not fed at regular intervals. In the first few days the dam will still be reluctant to get out of the box even for a drink, so you will need to offer her glucose water at regular intervals. Food should be offered little and often, and because her digestive system will be rather delicate for the first couple of days she should be kept on a light diet of chicken or fish (both carefully boned, of course) and I like to give one egg yolk, whisked with milk each day while she is still feeding the puppies. You will very probably have to coax her to eat during the first forty-eight hours and don't be afraid to hand-feed her if that is the only way you can get her to take food. As soon as the novelty of her puppies wears off slightly, her appetite will come back to normal and she will readily leave the whelping box to eat her meals when they arrive.

It is normal for the bitch to have a mucous discharge from the vulva after the puppies are born. For the first couple of days this will be malodorous and dark in colour, but the colour will then change to blood-red and will eventually pale off completely. This discharge is caused by bleeding from the surface of the uterus where the placentas have broken away. If the discharge remains thick and dark for more than a couple of days your vet should be consulted without delay.

The room housing the bitch and her puppies should be kept at a constant temperature of about 75 degrees fahrenheit, or it can be a little cooler, provided that an infra red lamp is being used to heat the whelping box itself. As I have already said, I prefer the latter arrangement for the bitch can be free to move to somewhere a little cooler when she is not in with her puppies, and if the lamp is situated off-centre she need not be in its direct rays. Most bitches will settle down perfectly contentedly at this early stage, but some can take time to adjust and will persist in moving their puppies about from place to place. Such bitches, which thankfully are in the minority, will need to be kept in the whelping box (making sure they are not too hot) and if they continue to be unsettled a vet should certainly be consulted. If you decide to weigh the puppies on a daily basis, this should be done while the bitch is out in the garden so that she does not have to witness any undue disturbance to her precious charges. Hopefully your puppies will all be putting on weight steadily (though there is frequently no increase during the first twenty-four hours) and if any do not appear to be thriving check that they are actually sucking, and not just sleeping contentedly attached to the teat. To help them on their way you can supplement their diet by hand-feeding and then let the bitch take over completely again when they have regained weight and strength, giving them ample opportunity to compete with the rest of the litter. You should expect each puppy to have doubled its birth weight within the first seven to ten days of its life. Thereafter a very general guide to weight gain is about six ounces per week.

When your bitch goes out for exercise be sure that she does not come into contact with any ground which might carry infection from other dogs. You can expect her motions to be somewhat loose for she will be cleaning up entirely after her puppies at this stage, licking tummy and anus to stimulate the flow of urine and bowel action. Always give her a quick check over before putting her back with her puppies, making sure that there are no signs of mastitis and that her discharge is clearing as expected. As the days progress she will tolerate little grooming sessions more readily, these are especially important if you have chosen to keep her in full coat for a tangled coat will increase the risk of tiny puppies getting trapped in it. Always keep some low level of light in the bitch's room throughout the night; this will enable her more easily to keep a check on the whereabouts of her puppies and will assist her if she needs to get out of the box for a drink or a snack during the night.

MUSCLE TWITCHING: Do not be disturbed by the fact that the puppies seem to twitch a lot. Ninety per cent of a new-born puppy's life is spent sleeping, and muscle twitching is perfectly normal at this time for it plays an essential part in the development of the muscles.

UMBILICAL CORDS: The umbilical cords should have dried up neatly within the first couple of days – they shrivel up and then fall off (possibly assisted by an over-indulgent dam!). If there is any sign of infection in the navel it should be bathed in a mild antiseptic and if it fails to clear up quickly, the vet should be consulted.

DEW CLAWS: Removal of dew claws on the Shih Tzu is optional, but if you decide to let the puppies keep them, they must be kept in trim. All puppy purchasers must be advised that dew claws are present, as they will not wear down naturally like the other nails on the feet. Buyers must be discouraged from having dew claws removed at a later stage, for this is entirely unnecessary (except in exceptional circumstances) and will involve a general anaesthetic which could otherwise be avoided. In recent years I have tended to leave dew claws on and have come across no problems whatsoever.

If you decide to have them removed, possibly because you are worried about injury by tearing (something more likely to happen in larger breeds) they must be removed by your vet when the puppies are three days old, and certainly no later than the fourth day. You may have heard it said that some breeders remove dew claws themselves, but this is a skilled operation which causes some pain, and it should only be done by a vet or a very experienced breeder. Unless the vet comes to your home, you will need to take the bitch along to the surgery with the puppies, for she will be frantic if they are taken away from her, even for a short period, at this stage. Travelling arrangements should be as described earlier, and once again it would be wise to give your vet a call to let him know that you are on your way. If you are worried about infection which may be picked up in the waiting room you can always wait outside in the car until it is your turn to see the vet. The bitch will have to be kept entirely out of ear-shot while the vet removes the claws for the enormous noise they make will disturb her considerably. Thankfully their agony is short-lived, and with potassium permanganate the bleeding is stopped almost instantly, so that they can go straight back to their dam.

EYES: The puppies will have been born with their eyes tightly closed, and they will remain like this for about the first ten days. The eyes will open of their own accord and on no account should they be forced, although if they are particularly sticky they may be bathed with a warm solution of very weak tea. At any sign of infection, contact your vet immediately. Once they are open, the eyes will be a misty blue in colour and they will not be able to focus properly. At this early stage the puppies should be kept away from bright light. The colour will clear and darken as the days progress.

EARS: At birth the ears will also be sealed and these will usually have opened by the thirteenth to seventeenth day.

NAILS: Puppies' nails are sharp and seem to grow extremely quickly. For the comfort of the dam, and as a measure of protection against injury to each other by accidental scratching, nails should be trimmed regularly with nail scissors.

PROBLEM PUPPIES

DEHYDRATION: Shih Tzu puppies should 'fill their skin'. This means that if you can feel an amount of loose flesh which, when grasped, does not spring back readily, especially at the back of the neck, the puppy could be dehydrating. This is cause for concern. If a puppy is limp when it is picked up, urgent attention is essential.

POOR SUCKERS: The crying of a puppy may be an indication that it is not getting sufficient milk. As has already been mentioned, the puppy will need individual attention, placing it on a teat about every two hours and checking that it is actually suckling. Supplementary hand-feeding may be necessary.

TOXIC MILK SUPPLY: This is indicated by puppies which cry more than normal. They may appear to be bloated and suffer from greenish-coloured diarrhoea, with a red swollen anus. Your vet should be consulted immediately and the puppies will very probably have to be hand-reared as infected milk is one of the causes of early death amongst puppies.

LACK OF STIMULATION: Another reason for a crying puppy can be that it needs to pass urine but has not been stimulated by the bitch to do so. You will have to stimulate the puppy on her behalf, simulating her washing action by rubbing the tummy and anus with a damp tissue. This will encourage the puppy to pass urine and to defaecate. It should be passed back to the bitch, rear-end first, and in most cases you will find that she will continue her maternal duties in the normal manner. In the unlikely event of having a bitch who is reluctant to clean up after her puppies, it will probably help if you smear a little vegetable oil on the puppies, giving her the stimulation to start cleaning them.

UMBILICAL HERNIAS: If present, these will probably already have been noticed. I have already mentioned that they can have been caused by an over-zealous dam and, if the hernia is small, it will probably close up with the passage of time. However, the majority of umbilical hernias are hereditary, and as the puppy grows the hernia will need to be checked by a vet to ascertain whether or not surgical rectification is necessary, for although many dogs can live a full life without any problem, there can be a danger of strangulation. Anyone who buys a puppy with a hernia should have the problem pointed out, and the full facts should be explained.

SUCKING DUE TO TEETHING: Puppies begin to teeth at around three weeks or sometimes earlier. At this time they will try to suck anything which is available, and their choice of object is not always the bitch's teat. Accidents can happen when puppies suck the limbs, ears and penises of their siblings, and they must be discouraged from doing this before damage occurs.

By the time the puppies have reached three weeks of age you should be handling them a great deal, and the bitch will hopefully not object to you doing so. This is the time when human contact is most important; it is also a particularly important week in their psychological development and should be free from unnecessary trauma. For this reason, providing that the bitch is coping adequately with her litter and is not being over-drained, I prefer to start weaning puppies in the fourth week. However, the bitch's well-being must be the first priority, and if she has a large litter or seems otherwise unable to cope, weaning must start sooner. There are a number of conditions which might affect the bitch, and will certainly influence your decision.

MASTITIS: Mastitis will first be observed by one of the teats becoming hot, hard or inflamed. It will be sore and the bitch may therefore be distressed. If this condition is caught in the early stages it may be rectified by holding a warm cloth over the affected teats and by trying to express a little of the milk by hand. If this appears to be working, hold the puppies to the affected teats and encourage them to use these teats rather than the others. If hardening continues and the matter is not resolved within the space of twelve hours, veterinary advice should be sought.

METRITIS: The first sign of metritis in a bitch is a lack of interest in her puppies and a certain lethargy. Metritis is an inflammation of the uterus, and the condition is usually caused by an unborn foetus or a retained placenta. If it is caught in sufficient time it can usually be rectified with a course of antibiotics. If the bitch is not treated her milk will become toxic, and the puppies will have to be hand-reared. The condition can be fatal, and in severe cases, or the occasional case when the bitch does not respond to treatment, spaying may be necessary. Metritis can also be caused by bacteria introduced into the genital tract, possibly by the use of unclean fingers used to aid a difficult whelping, or from unclean bedding. Scrupulous cleanliness is therefore essential.

ECLAMPSIA: I find eclampsia one of the most frightening things which can happen to a bitch, for it can occur within such a short period of time and death can occur within the space of a few hours. This is why it is essential to have sufficient time to spend with a bitch and her litter; you cannot hold down full time employment while attempting to raise a litter. In humans this condition is known as 'milk fever'. It is often thought to be caused by lack of calcium, but in fact it is due to the body's inability to transport the calcium from the body reserves into the bloodstream.

It is easy to miss the first outward signs of eclampsia: the bitch may seem a little strange, and she might start nest-making, scratching up her bedding, much as she did before whelping commenced. As the condition progresses she will seem uneasy, restless and on edge, probably panting more than usual. If you place your hands on her shoulder blades at this stage you may be able to perceive a slight tremble which will soon develop into a shiver. Her legs will stiffen and she will begin to wobble about and have difficulty in standing. As her condition worsens her pulse will become rapid and she will salivate, eventually going into convulsions, by which time her temperature will have risen to as much as 104 degrees (41 degrees C).

The only way to save the bitch is by a massive dose of calcium given intravenously by your vet, so whatever the time of day or night, do not delay. Ring the vet at once, telling him of your suspicion of eclampsia, and let him know that you are on your way to the surgery as a matter of urgency. Once he has administered the calcium your bitch will most probably seem to recover almost immediately, but that does not mean that she can necessarily continue to feed her puppies as she did before. On this matter you will have to take your vet's advice, and this may vary depending on the severity of her previous condition, and the age and size of the litter of puppies. He may say that she cannot feed them at all, or he may give strict instruction as to the maximum amount of time she can spend with the puppies each day, for if she is taken away from them completely, it will cause her great distress. In this case it will very probably be necessary to supplement the puppies' feeds. Even if your vet permits her to continue feeding, it would be advisable to commence weaning as soon as possible. If the bitch is to remain with her puppies without feeding them, it is possible to use a stocking with holes cut out for the four legs, thereby covering her teats and preventing their accessibility. However, I have not used this myself so I cannot vouch for its success.

By about three weeks of age the puppies should be up on their feet and be starting to move around – their confidence will be growing daily. They will need a little more space, although they should still be kept safely enclosed so that they are out of harm's way. Electric cables, for example, can be lethal if a puppy decides to exercise its new teeth on the rubbery taste of the outer casing! The dam will probably choose to spend a little more time away from her litter, signifying that it is time for you to take over their general care and feeding. Once the puppies are introduced to solid foods she will no longer clean up after them, and the dirty work will be left entirely to you. This is when your work really begins. You will need to try to encourage the puppies to urinate and defaecate outside their sleeping quarters, which they usually like to keep reasonably clean. I cover only half the surface of the whelping box with bedding, leaving just a good supply of newspaper on the other half. I usually find that in most cases (there are always exceptions!) they use the newspaper which, of course, needs to be changed with great regularity.

WEANING
Every breeder has personal preferences as to the most successful way to wean, and I am sure that we all experiment with new feeding products from time to time. There are now some excellent proprietary puppy feeds on the market and if you choose to use these I do feel it must be stressed that they are to be used strictly according to the maker's instructions. It is also important to select a brand which you know you can get hold of easily, or else you should buy a large enough supply to last until the puppies are at least several weeks old. Changing the type of food given during the weaning process can cause havoc, and will almost certainly cause upset tummies.

It is much easier to commence weaning when the puppies' tummies are empty and they therefore feel hungry. For this reason, do not offer the food when they are wide awake and have probably fed from their dam, wait until they wake from a nice long sleep, undoubtedly feeling hungry. I find that the ideal feeding bowl is shallow, but large enough for all the puppies to get their heads into without having to push one another out of the way. Of course, it must be a bowl

Three young Bellakerne puppies at three weeks of age.   *T. Richardson.*

which is easy to clean thoroughly, my own preference is for stainless steel. The first feed is almost always a bit of a performance, for almost certainly one little fellow will decide to walk into the bowl while you are concentrating on someone else! However, I do find that those who commence weaning at four weeks take to it with rather more of a professional attitude than youngsters of only three weeks. However, after the first few feeds all the puppies seem to know exactly what they are doing and look forward to their mealtimes with relish.

I use the following weaning schedule, and it seems to work well. In the early stages the puppies will continue to feed from their dam between meals, but their need to do this should wane as the weeks progress.

DAY ONE: Introduce one milk feed around lunchtime, this should be a rather 'sloppy' mixture of porridge or good quality oats with warm goat's milk and a teaspoonful of clear honey. It is not advisable to change from one kind of milk to another, so if fresh goat's milk is not readily available, it is worth knowing that it freezes well and can often be purchased pre-frozen from health food stores. Alternatively, there are several good proprietary milk mixes, but take care to select one designed especially for puppies and mix exactly as per the instructions.

DAY TWO: Feed a milk meal (as above) at lunchtime and another milk meal (also as above) just before bedtime. This will prevent the puppies from taking too much from the bitch during the night.

DAY THREE: Give a milk feed as soon as the puppies wake up in the morning, before they have had time to feed from the dam. At lunchtime introduce their first meat meal of a well-soaked puppy feed (put it through a blender for the first few days) with a top quality brand of canned puppy meat, which is very well mashed. Another milk feed should be given just before bedtime.

DAY FOUR AND ONWARDS: Breakfast and lunch should be as per day three. Next give a milk feed in the late afternoon and another meat meal last thing at night, establishing a pattern of milk, meat, milk, meat.

It is really not possible to be specific about quantities, it will obviously vary according to the number and size of the puppies, and the bitch's own milk supply. If the puppies do not clean up their bowl at each feed it is much better to feed a little less at each meal, rather than to reduce the schedule to three meals. The bitch will gradually be spending longer and longer away from her charges, and she will most probably do this of her own choosing. If she is reluctant to leave them you will need to encourage her to be away from them in order that her milk supply begins to dry up. The puppies should be completely weaned by about seven weeks of age so that they are capable of looking after themselves by the time they move on to their new homes. You will need to slowly reduce your bitch's intake of food, but it must still be of the very highest quality. Her coat may well have suffered greatly as a result of her litter, and a little cod-liver oil added to her diet will help to improve this.

WEIGHT GUIDE

Shih Tzu puppies vary in weight quite considerably, but most reach roughly half their adult weight by the age of four months. A puppy of this age should weigh between 5 and 8lb. By six months the puppy will be about two-thirds of its adult weight, so 71/2 to 12lb. is about the norm.

WORMING

Even though you will have wormed your bitch shortly prior to mating, there is still a possibility that the puppies will have worms because the worm ova can be passed from the dam, via the placenta, to the unborn whelps. A worming programme should commence at about four weeks of age, and the dam should also be wormed at this time.

Chapter Eleven

HEALTH PROBLEMS
AND AGEING

ABSCESS There is always a danger that an abscess may not be caught it its early stages because it goes undetected under the Shih Tzu's profuse coat. An abscess is very painful and should be bathed gently in a solution of hot salt-water. This will bring it to a head and it should burst, thereby releasing the pus content and allowing it to drain. Bathing must, however, be continued after the abscess has burst, for it needs to drain completely and the skin must therefore not be allowed to heal too quickly. If the abscess fails to burst, or if more than one appears, you will need to consult your vet who will most probably recommend a course of antibiotics. Abscesses can appear virtually anywhere, including on the anus. One of the most frequent causes is a fight with another dog, where a slight nick of the skin has gone undetected.

ALOPECIA This occurs when old hair drops out prematurely, before the new hair has grown in. It can be caused by a change in hormonal balance and is frequently found in bitches who are rearing or have recently reared puppies. A course of cortisone or steroids can also cause the hair to fall out quite dramatically. If the cause is not known veterinary advice must be sought, for it can be associated with a variety of disorders including skin conditions.

ANAL GLANDS All dogs have anal glands, located on either side of the anal aperture, and it is possible for a Shih Tzu to go throughout its life without having them emptied, although, as I mentioned earlier, I feel it is wise to check them from time to time. A Shih Tzu which scoots along the ground, rubbing the anus, probably has full glands which need to be emptied. Unless you are confident that you can do this yourself with ease, you should go to the vet for what is usually a very simple and painless procedure.

CONSTIPATION This can be caused by diet, so it is often possible to cure the problem by altering the feeding programme. If you offer dry biscuit meal, try giving it soaked, and if you feed canned meats you could try including some chopped green vegetables, cooked in lightly salted water. As a temporary measure only, you could offer a meal of uncooked red meat or liver without any biscuit content. If you feed bones (something I do not recommend) there is a chance that pieces of chipped bone may have caused a blockage. A teaspoon of olive oil may be given as an initial measure, but if constipation persists your vet will have to examine your Shih Tzu so that the cause can be determined.

COPROPHAGY (EATING OF FAECES) Occasionally a bitch can develop this habit after raising a litter, but it usually manifests itself when a Shih Tzu is still in the puppy stage. It is a most unpleasant habit, and although it is often said that coprophagy is carried out to offset a lack of protein, vitamins or minerals in the diet, it can also be present in dogs which are fed a perfectly balanced diet. There seems to be no certain remedy but putting a little fat or treacle in the diet has been said to help. It goes without saying that the habit should be strongly discouraged and that faeces should be removed as soon as they are deposited in order to remove the temptation.

DANDRUFF Dandruff or mild dry skin conditions can often be solved by the addition of a little oil in the diet. Try mixing a little vegetable oil in each meal, and this will very probably lessen the problem. Should it persist, veterinary advice will have to be sought as there may be an underlying skin condition which will have to be treated professionally.

DEAFNESS Congenital deafness does not seem to be a prevalent problem in the Shih Tzu, but full or partial deafness can occur as a degeneration due to the aging process. It is not always easy to assess but it can usually be tested by clapping your hands when the dog is not looking and observing the response. Don't clap too close to the dog for it may pick up the current of air which could give you a false impression of the severity of its impediment.

DIARRHOEA This can be caused by a slight chill or a change of diet, in which case it would be wise to offer cooled, boiled water, mixed with a little glucose powder. Your Shih Tzu should be kept on a light diet of fish or white meat for a while, and arrowroot can also be of assistance. However, diarrhoea can also be a sign of much more serious trouble so if your dog seems to be feeling unwell, lacks appetite or has any evidence of blood in the motions you should seek immediate veterinary advice and isolate it from other dogs.

DRY EYE This is a drying of the surface of the cornea and is caused by an insufficiency of lacrimal gland secretion. It can eventually result in conjunctivitis and keratitis in one or both eyes. 'Dry-eye' can follow infection or injury to the lacrimal gland or its nerve. As with any eye problem, early veterinary advice should be sought. As an aid to keeping the eye moist, special eye drops may be given on a regular basis to alleviate the problem.

EAR INFECTIONS Because hair grows very deep inside the ear of the long-coated Shih Tzu, ear infections can set up very easily. For this reason always keep a careful check for any excess build-up of wax or ear mites which can both give rise to canker. When grooming your dog you should automatically check the ears. If there is any sign of a foul-smelling discharge, possibly in an ear which is red and hot to the touch, you should seek veterinary advice immediately. Ear infections are painful and will almost certainly cause the dog to scratch the ear, thus increasing the irritation. A dog with an ear infection may also shake its head and hold the head on one side, usually with the affected ear downwards.

EYE DAMAGE The eyes of the Shih Tzu do have a tendency to discharge a little, but if they do so more than normally or if they are excessively watery, check to see that nothing is aggravating the eye. There is always the danger of, for example, a small piece of grit becoming lodged in the eye or the eye might be scratched in a fight or in play. Simple cases usually respond to antibiotic treatment, but prompt attention to eye injuries is important. If your vet prescribes an eye ointment hold the nozzle a little away from the eye and squeeze the ointment into the inner corner. Then close the eyelids together gently with your fingers to distribute the ointment over the eye. If you are using eye drops, which are usually easier to administer, be careful not to let the dropper touch the eye.

FOREIGN BODIES LODGED IN THE MOUTH A dog which has difficulty closing its mouth, is constantly pawing at it or is salivating heavily, may have something wedged between its teeth or even across the roof of its mouth, between the upper molars. If you are unable to dislodge this yourself with relative ease, consult your vet straight away for, apart from the obvious discomfort to the dog, inflammation will almost certainly result.

FUNGUS Dogs which are prone to lying around on damp grass or in other damp places often get a minute fungus which appears as little black spots, usually around the nipples or where there is no coat. This can cause irritation and can be cured by wiping with a solution made up by your chemist of one part chloroform to two parts alcohol. Two applications with a few days gap in between usually clears up the problem.

FUR BALLS Because it is a long-coated breed the Shih Tzu can be prone to fur balls. These can come about from coat that is taken into the mouth when dogs are playing with each other, or from a dog licking its own fur. Occasionally a Shih Tzu will vomit a fur ball without any fuss or bother, and without previously having shown any sign of illness or discomfort. Fur balls, however, must never be regarded lightly as they can cause a dog to choke.

HAY FEVER Dogs can have an allergy to pollens just as humans do, and this will be displayed by excessive watering of the eyes and sneezing due to inflammation of the mucous membranes within the nose. Finding the best form of relief for your Shih Tzu is rarely easy but your vet, often by trial and error, can usually find something which will help to alleviate the problem.

HEART PROBLEMS It is rare to find a dog dying suddenly from a 'heart attack' as we know it in humans, but dogs suffering from heart disease, especially when there is an obstruction in the flow of blood to the brain, may collapse, becoming limp and unconscious. Frequently in such cases the dog will recover within a matter of seconds, when it will need to be given fresh air. In coronary cases (i.e. poor blood supply to the heart muscle) the type of collapse is different as the limbs usually remain stiff and the dog does not lose consciousness. The latter is not particularly common in dogs, but there do appear to be instances of heart disease in the Shih Tzu, not all of which are inherited. An older Shih Tzu may suffer from a weakening of the heart, indicated by a hard cough and lethargy, breathing becoming more rapid than usual. If veterinary advice is sought in good time the problem may well be held at bay with a course of tablets and a controlled diet.

HEATSTROKE Extreme care must be taken not to leave dogs where they will be exposed to excessive heat. It is surprising how quickly heat builds up in a so-called 'ventilated' car, even on a relatively mild day. Time is of the essence when treating heatstroke. The dog should be placed in the cool, and iced or very cold water should be liberally applied to head, neck and shoulders. If the dog is unconscious no attempt must be made to get it to take a drink, but once it has regained consciousness, and only then, it can be offered glucose water or a light saline solution.

INGUINAL HERNIA These hernias, located in the groin area, can be found in both dogs and bitches, and in one groin or in both. Sometimes they will not become apparent until the dog is well into adulthood. Veterinary advice should always be sought in order to determine whether surgical correction is necessary. No Shih Tzu which has this problem should be used for breeding purposes.

KENNEL COUGH There are many different forms of kennel cough, all of which are highly contagious. The first sign of this viral infection is that the dog seems to be trying to clear its throat, and it is easy to think at first that it has something stuck in its throat. This uncomfortable noise gradually progresses to a hoarse cough. Veterinary treatment must be sought immediately, but do not take your dog into the vet's waiting room. Kennel cough is highly infectious and your Shih Tzu must be isolated from all other dogs, not only while it is coughing, but for a good few weeks afterwards. Kennel cough can lead to bronchitis, and is more dangerous in young puppies, older dogs and those with a heart condition. Kennel cough vaccines are now available, and you would be well advised to check that some measure of protection is included when your dog receives other vaccinations. Some vets now include this as a matter of course.

KIDNEY FAILURE Primary signs of kidney failure are excessive thirst with the resultant frequent passing of water, breathing may become accelerated and the dog may appear to age prematurely. Unfortunately kidney disorders do occasionally appear in young stock and it is possible that such problems are inherited.

LAMENESS One of the most likely causes of sudden lameness in a Shih Tzu is a clump of hair which has wedged between the pads, having gone unnoticed during grooming. The hair may have formed into a hard ball which presses into the foot when the dog walks on it. In this case the tight knot must be very carefully removed with scissors. A foreign object such as a tiny stone can also become wedged and can cause a dog to suddenly become lame. Check that the lameness is not caused by nails that are too long. Of course, there can be many other, more complex, reasons for dogs becoming lame so if the problem cannot be solved after careful inspection of the pads your vet should be consulted.

LIVER DISEASES All liver problems are serious, so your vet should always be contacted at the very first sign of any disorder. A symptom which you will notice with relative ease is a jaundiced yellowing of the white of the eye and of the membranes lining the eye and the mouth. You may also notice a yellowing on the underside of the ear flap, less easy to detect in artificial light than in daylight. Other symptoms include sickness, loss of appetite, constipation and infrequent passing of highly coloured urine.

POISONING The initial signs of poisoning are various, but they can include sudden vomiting, muscular spasms and, in the case of warfarin poisoning, bleeding from an exit point such as the gums. The antidote used will depend upon the type of poison taken, and remember that a dog can not only eat poison but can also walk on it and lick it from its pads. Seek veterinary treatment immediately and, if possible, give the vet details of the type of poison your dog has come into contact with. When you telephone your vet take his advice as to whether vomiting should be induced, for it is not recommended for all types of poisoning. Make sure you keep your Shih Tzu warm and quiet, and let it have some fresh air.

PUFFS There may be a technical name for this, but if so, I have never discovered it! It is not usually a major problem, but it can be frightening for the new owner to experience for the first time. It is caused by an elongation of the soft palate, and is more likely to occur in the brachycephalic (short-nosed) breeds. The dog will suddenly draw in short, sharp breaths through the nostrils or mouth, it usually looks rather tense, standing four-square and with its head thrust forward. This does not happen in all Shih Tzu, but it can be brought on when the dog becomes very excited. This 'puffing' will usually only last for a few seconds or perhaps a minute, but you can stop it immediately by putting your fingers over the dog's nostrils, thereby causing it to breathe only through the mouth – a quick and simple solution to this little problem. Of course, there can be other reasons for a dog puffing, such as a grass seed in the nasal cavity. If you suspect that the problem is anything more serious than the 'puffs' you must consult your vet.

SALIVARY FAILURE If a dog is a poor eater it can, just occasionally, be due to the fact that it is not producing enough saliva. If you put a small, tasty morsel of food into the mouth it will sometimes activate the salivary glands, thus stimulating the desire to eat.

SCRATCHING This can be due to an incorrect diet, possibly including a surfeit of dairy products or too high a protein content, especially in the summer months when the Shih Tzu can become over-heated. Too much oil in the diet can be another cause, so you would be wise to consider the diet carefully and reduce whatever is most likely to be causing the problem. Scratching can, of course, be caused by a number of other things. In a long-coated breed you must take especial care that your Shih Tzu is not affected by fleas or other parasites. Bathing your dogs in an insecticidal shampoo should keep parasites at bay, but other preparations can also be obtained, preferably from your vet. If harvest mites are prevalent in your area, it would be wise to dip the feet in permanganate of potash before walking where mites might be picked up. A dog which scratches behind its ear, often making a rather vocal 'whining' noise, may well have an ear infection. Again, your vet should be consulted as to the most appropriate treatment.

SHEEP TICKS Sheep ticks can, unfortunately, be picked up not only from sheep themselves, but also from the grass where they have been grazing. If you walk your dog in sheep country you must be especially vigilant in checking its coat and skin when you return home. A sheep tick will, at first glance, look rather like a dark blue wart which will increase in size as the tick, whose head is embedded in the dog's skin, sucks on the blood. Ticks cause great irritation, and your dog will probably let you know it has a problem by constantly scratching and nibbling at the affected area. The safest way to remove a tick is the application of salt on the tick, but you must be sure that the head is fully removed or infection could cause an abscess to form. If you merely try to pull off the tick you stand a very good chance of removing the body without the head.

SNEEZING The cause of your dog sneezing must always be looked into urgently, for it can be a sign of serious disease such as distemper. However, it can also signify that the membranes within the nose are inflamed, possibly due to an irritant such as a grass seed, perhaps a slight injury or even a parasite. Sneezing can also be the result of hay fever. If sneezing persists, a vet must be consulted without delay.

SPINAL DISORDERS Because the Shih Tzu is a short-legged, reasonably long dog, you must be on the alert for back problems. Care should be taken when dogs jump on and off furniture, particularly if it is an older dog. At any sign of spinal injury, consult your vet at once. Sometimes it is possible for the dog to recover, seemingly completely, but in other cases partial paralysis may result.

STINGS Any dog which is stung in the mouth or on the throat should be attended to by a vet at once, and an anti-histamine injection must be administered. Keep the dog cool, and try to keep the tongue forward so that the airway remains clear. Perhaps the most usual place for a sting is in the pad of the foot and this is much less serious, albeit no less painful. TCP will usually bring some relief and vinegar is particularly good for wasp stings. Bicarbonate of soda can be applied to bee stings when the sting has been removed with tweezers.

TIGHT NOSTRILS This appears to be an inherited condition in the Shih Tzu and can be apparent either at birth or between ten days and about three weeks of age. There are instances of this condition not becoming evident until around the age of eight weeks. When seen at birth, the nostril is so tight that it is deformed; it is curved inwards and clearly highly undesirable. In other cases the nostrils are sufficiently wide at birth but later begin to tighten, possibly because of a variable growth rate in the puppy. Mucous membranes become swollen and the puppy seems unable to smell, often refusing to suckle, even when near the teats. Because the puppy cannot breathe through its nostrils, it holds its head up with its mouth open, and cries continuously because it is distressed. Urgent attention is necessary for it will almost certainly grow weak and die if left to its own devices. It will need to be kept warm and to be hand-fed hourly, with a puppy rearing formula. Mrs Dadds, in her highly informative book, *The Shih Tzu*, recommends adding a teaspoon of brandy to one cup of feed. Even if the puppy is put back with the dam and starts to suckle, it may yet again go into relapse and will therefore need constant attention. Usually this condition lasts only up to fourteen days. In those cases where the nostrils appear normal until the puppy is a couple of months old the problem often fails to rectify itself until the second teeth have been cut. Keeping the affected puppy's environment at a constant temperature seems to be of assistance.

TOOTH PROBLEMS The shorter-nosed breeds are prone to losing their incisor teeth sooner than those with a longer foreface and scissor bite. It is also likely that those puppies which develop their teeth later than the majority have a tendency to lose them sooner, possibly because the teeth are more shallowly rooted. Often a tooth can be lost without any apparent distress to the dog and without the owner even noticing until grooming up for the next show! To help avoid decay the teeth should be kept free from tartar. If you are not proficient in keeping your dog's teeth tartar-free yourself, your vet will usually be quite willing to carry out a scale and polish. A dog which is suffering from toothache will usually rub its head constantly along the ground and may be reluctant to eat. Some swelling may also be noticed.

TRAVEL SICKNESS Many Shih Tzu never suffer from travel sickness at all, but others unfortunately are prone to this problem. You will know when your dog is a puppy whether or not it will suffer in this way, and it will often overcome the problem as it matures. Travel sickness can display itself simply as excessive dribbling or a dog can throw up all the way to a show! Mercifully there are now some extremely good canine travel sickness tablets on the market, available from good pet stores or from stalls at dog shows.

UMBILICAL HERNIAS (See Chapter Ten concerning whelping and weaning). Just occasionally a rather different type of 'hernia', also located in the umbilical area, can come much later in the life of a bitch which has undergone a caesarian operation. This is a result of an adhesion on the scar tissue and medical advice must be sought as to whether or not removal is necessary.

UNDESCENDED TESTICLES When neither testicle descends in a male Shih Tzu, it is known as a cryptorchid, and if only one is descended, it is a unilateral-cryptorchid. Technically the common term 'monorchid' should be applied to dogs which only possess one testicle. In the Shih Tzu the testicles have usually descended fully by the age of six months and often very much sooner. In the majority of cases cryptorchidism (and monorchidism) is hereditary and breeding from such stock is definitely not to be recommended; such a dog may, however, be capable of reproducing. In any event, veterinary advice should be sought, for there is a risk of a tumour forming in a testicle which is retained.

VOMITING A Shih Tzu may vomit a clear, white or yellowish bile from time to time, usually due to a mild gastric irritation or indigestion. It can be helpful to starve the dog for twenty-four hours, offering just cooled, boiled water with a little glucose powder added. Constant vomiting of any kind, or vomiting with evidence that your dog feels unwell, are cause for a visit to the vet.

THE ELDERLY SHIH TZU

A Shih Tzu often lives for a good few years more than many breeds of dog, several making it to the age of sixteen years, and twenty plus is not unknown. Without doubt, if you care for your canine companions you will wish to give them every comfort they deserve in their closing years. Be sure that they have adequate warmth, high quality food, and that they are exercised sensibly. If you normally feed only one meal daily you would be well advised to split this into two smaller meals as an aid to digestion and also to give another 'highlight' to the day. Do not allow an 'oldie' to become overweight, remembering that older dogs have a tendency to put on weight more easily than youngsters. Excess weight will put undue pressure on the heart, and this is often detected by an unpleasant cough. Weight can, of course, also have an adverse effect on various other organs and on the limbs. A cough can also be a sign of worms, and it is wise to keep all your dogs wormed regularly, the older ones on an annual basis. If, however, your older dog is in ill health, take your vet's advice before worming.

Do not subject your older dog to lengthy grooming sessions, but keep them regular and fairly short. Make every effort to prevent the dog getting damp or cold, and after bathing make sure that it is kept in a pleasantly warm temperature for a good while afterwards. If teeth have been lost or have become loosened, you will need to take more care as to the consistency of the foods you offer, but do not deprive your Shih Tzu of all its much-loved chewy things, for it is surprising how a dog without any incisors left in its head can thoroughly enjoy a good chew with its back teeth. Just use your commonsense, and avoid anything which it seems unable to manage. It may be a good idea to use a puppy meal instead of the slightly larger biscuit meal you usually feed, and if you feed proprietary canned dog food (one of the better quality ones, of course), you may consider serving the puppy variety which will be of a more manageable consistency. Naturally, if your dog has a medical condition which requires a special diet your veterinary surgeon will advise what is best, often recommending one of the high-quality low-protein diets now available. If teeth are badly decayed they will need to be surgically removed, but I am always rather cautious about a general anaesthetic given to an older dog, so try to keep the teeth in good condition so as to avoid the necessity for this.

If sight is failing avoid moving furniture and your dog's own personal items more than is necessary. In this way it will be able to get used to exactly where thing are, so that it still feels fairly confident, mishaps and accidents being kept to a minimum. An ageing dog can sometimes have difficulty in controlling its waterworks. This can be for a variety of reasons, and if this problem occurs you will need to consult your vet to determine the cause. Do not scold the older dog severely for accidents of this nature; there will almost certainly be a medical reason for a 'clean' dog having accidents. It would be wise to leave a thick wad of newspaper by the door in the hope that it will use this if you are not going to be around to let it out when nature calls. If your vet asks for a urine sample for analysis, try to obtain the first urine of the day. Do not spend hours trying to get the prospective patient to aim straight into the little sterilized bottle you intend to give to the vet, but catch the urine in a sterilized, stainless steel container and then pour this into the bottle – this is much the easiest way to go about this difficult procedure.

I always used to advise that a young puppy should not be introduced to live with an older dog, and whether or not this is considered, is very much dependent upon the personality of the older dog, its ailments and your own domestic circumstances. Undoubtedly a youngster must only be kept with a veteran under constant supervision, and the old dog must have plenty of time to itself so that it can rest when needed. In my own case, I have successfully allowed an ageing dog to live with a youngster, although only for a few hours a day. I found it gave the older dog added interest, and the enjoyment derived from the youngster's company in those closing months of life were a pleasure to see. Naturally, if you do keep young and old dogs together you need to be ultra-cautious for the sake of both puppy and older dog, particular care must be taken to ensure that the old fellow does not snap and injure the youngster. Most important of all, never let the older dog feel that its nose has been pushed out to make way for the youngster. It must be made to feel just as important as it has always been, and, what is more, it needs to have that little bit of extra attention to make it feel even more special. As in all aspects of kennel management, so much comes down to pure, basic, commonsense.

TIME TO PART

Sooner or later the dreaded time comes around. If you are lucky your old dog will die peacefully in its sleep without pain, sparing you the anguish of wondering whether or not the time has come to take the decision of putting it out of any misery it may be suffering. Thankfully vets are able to prescribe some excellent pain-killing drugs so that in many cases a dog can have a major and terminal illness without suffering unnecessarily. But when the pain killers no longer have sufficient effect, or if your dog is no longer able to live in comfort and with dignity, the time has come to part.

Having a dog put to sleep brings with it inevitable distress to the owner, but try not to show the dog how upset you are; there will be plenty of time for tears after it has gone. If possible, choose a vet with whom both you and the dog are familiar. The vet will usually visit your home if you wish, or you can take your Shih Tzu along to the surgery. If your dog has established a friendly rapport with your vet over the years it will probably go into the surgery expecting its usual routine check. If it is suffering it will very probably associate the surgery with the place it goes to when it is in pain, after which that pain is relieved. And that is just the way it will be. If you feel you can keep control of your emotions in front of your beloved pet, stay with it while it is injected so that it has your reassurance as it goes finally to sleep. That sleep comes quickly and almost imperceptibly. Do try not to let your dog down at the last, for it has undoubtedly given you many long years of faithful service.

After it has gone the vet will take charge of the disposal of the body if you wish, or provided there is no serious risk of infection, you may have the body to bury, perhaps in its favourite spot in the garden. There are, incidentally, some special metal trunks available for the purpose should you so wish. Those who neither wish to leave their dog with the vet nor have it buried in the garden can take advantage of one of the commercial pet cemeteries, details of which are usually available from your vet. Arrangements will be made through your vet for your dog to be collected and taken to the 'cemetery' where it can be either cremated or buried. The ashes can be scattered in the cemetery gardens, a plaque erected or a shrub planted in your dog's memory. Alternatively, you may have the ashes returned to you. It will be appreciated that there is a fairly substantial charge for this service, but most services also offer the option of having your pet cremated with others in order to keep the cost lower. While we are discussing this unhappy but inevitable subject, readers might also like to consider making some provision for their Shih Tzu should the owner depart this world first. Speak to your solicitor about how the dogs can be included in your will, for by doing so, you will feel comfortable in your own mind that the four-legged friends who have shared your hearth will be taken care of in the manner you feel will be best for them.

It seems sad to close a book on the unhappy subject of parting, but I, personally, believe that the end of a life is just as important as the beginning. In any event, it is my earnest wish that you and your Shih Tzu enjoy each other's company for many thoroughly enjoyable years.

APPENDICES

Appendix I

SELECTED BIBLIOGRAPHY

Ash, Edward C - Dogs and Their History, Vol 2, Ernest Benn, 1927

Ash, Edward C - This Doggie Business, Hutchinson & Co, 1934

Avedon, John - In Exile From the Land of Snows, Wisdom Publications, 1985

Bailey, Lieut.-Col F M - No Passport to Tibet, Rupert Hart-Davis, 1957

Bell, Sir Charles - Portrait of the Dalai Lama, Collins, 1946

Bylandt, Count H de - Dogs of All Nations, Kegan Paul & Co, 1904

Carmello and Battagalia, Dr and L - Dog Genetics - How to Breed Better Dogs, TFH Publications Inc., 1978

Collier, V W F - Dogs of China and Japan in Nature and in Art - Heinemann, 1921

Croxton Smith, A - Dogs Since 1900, Non Sporting Breeds - Some Far Eastern Dogs, Andrew Dakers, 1950

Cunliffe, Juliette - All About The Lhasa Apso - Pelham, 1990

Cutting, Suydam - The Fire Ox and Other Years, Charles Scribner's Sons, 1940

Dadds, Audrey - The Shih Tzu - Popular Dogs, 1974

Dale-Green, Patricia - Dog, Rupert Hart-Davis, 1966

David-Neel, Alexandra - With Mystics and Magicians in Tibet, Penguin Books, 1931

Dixey, Annie Coath - The Lion Dog of Peking - Latimer Trend & Co, 1931

Easton, Rev D Allan and Brearley, Joan McDonald - This Is The
    Shih Tzu - T F H Publications, N.D.

Frankling, Eleanor (Revised by Trevor Turner, BVetMed, MRCVS) - Practical Dog Breeding and Genetics, Popular Dogs, 1981

Gelder, Stuart and Roma - The Timely Rain, Hutchinson & Co Ltd, 1964

Godden, Rumer - The Butterfly Lions, The Pekingese in History, Legend and Art - Macmillan London Limited, 1977

Harrer, Heinrich - Seven Years in Tibet, Rupert Hart-Davis, 1955

Harrer, Heinrich - Return to Tibet, Pinguin-Verlag, 1983

Hubbard, Clifford L B - Dogs in Britain, Macmillan & Co Ltd., 1948

Hutchinson, W (Ed) - Hutchinson's Popular Illustrated Dog Encyclopaedia, 1933-1934

Johnson, Norman H - The Complete Book of Dogs, Robert Hayle & Co, 1965

Legl-Jacobsson, Elizabeth - East Asiatic Breeds, Tryck Produktion, Sweden, 1978

Lu Zee Yuen Nee, Madam - The Lhassa Lion Dog - (translation by Chow Sze King) - The Peking Kennel Club, 1935

Migot, Andre - Tibetan Marches, Rupert Hart-Davis, 1955

Richards, Dr Herbert - Dog Breeding For Professionals, THF Publications, 1978

Simsova, Sylvia - Tibetan and Related Dog Breeds, A Guide to Their History, Tibetan Terrier Association, 1979

Seranne, Ann with Miller, Lise M - The Joy of Owning a Shih Tzu, Howell Book House Inc., 1983

Sloan and Farquhar, A and A - Dog and Man, The Story of a Friendship, George H Doran Company, 1925

Turner, Trevor BVet Med, MRCVS (Ed) - Veterinary Notes for Dog Owners, Popular Dogs, 1990

Vesey-Fitzgerald, Brian - The Domestic Dog, Routledge & Kegan Paul Ltd, 1957

West, Geoffrey, MRCVS - All About Your Dog's Health, Pelham Books, 1979

West, Stanley - The Book of Dogs, Alexander Ousley Ltd, 1935

White, Kay - Dogs, Their Mating Whelping and Weaning, K & R Books Ltd, 1977

Widdrington, Gay - The Shih Tzu Handbook - 1971

Wynyard, Ann Lindsay - Dog Directory Guide to Owning a Tibetan Spaniel, The Dog Directory, 1980

Wynyard, Ann Lindsay, Dogs of Tibet and the History of the Tibetan Spaniel, Book World, Rugby, 1982

OTHER PUBLICATIONS

Club des Chiens du Tibet (France) - Newsletters
Dog World
Kennel Gazette
Manchu Shih Tzu Society Newsletters and Book of Champions
Northern Counties Shih Tzu Club - British Shih Tzu Champions -
Northern Counties Shih Tzu Club - European Year Book - articles by Kiskova and Kourilova Zdena, Frances Hickey, Eija Verlander, Carola Vorderstemann, Kristian Hansen, Bodil Fossenius, Walter Holtorf, Kirsten and Preben Larsen, the Swedish Shih Tzu Club and Club des Chiens Tibetains de France.
Our Dogs
Shih Tzu News

Appendix II

CHINESE DYNASTIES FROM THE THIRTEENTH CENTURY

Yuan (Mongol)	1280 - 1368
Ming	1368 - 1644
Ch'ing (Manchu)	1644 - 1912

EMPERORS OF THE MANCHU DYNASTY

Shun-chih	1644 - 1661
K'ang-hsi	1662 - 1722
Yung-cheng	1723 - 1735
Ch'ien-lung	1736 - 1795
Chaia-ch'ing	1796 - 1821
Tao-kuang	1821 - 1850
Hsien-feng	1851 - 1861
T'ung-chih	1862 - 1873
Kuang-hsu	1874 - 1907
Hsuan-t'ung	1908 - 1912

Appendix III

UK KENNEL CLUB REGISTRATIONS FOR SHIH TZU

Year	Registrations	Year	Registrations
1934	39	1951	60
1935	20	1952	53
1936	31	1953	41
1937	18	1954	71
1938	28	1955	80
1939	47	1956	97
1940	11	1957	110
1941	11	1958	132
1942	7	1959	133
1943	2	1960	153
1944	12	1961	226
1945	3	1962	276
1946	5	1963	355
1947	10	1964	447
1948	28	1965	499
1949	42	1966	498
1950	40	1967	540

Year	Registrations	Year	Registrations
1968	771	1980	1823
1969	1037	1981	1528
1970	1526	1982	1397
1971	1453	1983	1425
1972	1441	1984	1531
1973	1583	1985	1576
1974	1940	1986	1532
1975	1613	1987	1743
1976	937*	1988	1755
1977	716*	1989	3898
1978	1380*	1990	4603
1979	2013	1991	4426

*For the years 1976, 1977 and 1978 there are no total registration figures available as at that time the Kennel Club operated a two-tier system. The figures given here are those on the active register, i.e. registered with the intention of being shown.

Appendix IV

BRITISH BREED CLUBS

THE SHIH TZU CLUB

The Shih Tzu (Tibetan Lion Dog) Club was the first to be founded for the breed, application being made in 1934 to change the title from Apso and Lion Dog Club. In 1934 the title of the Club was finally altered to Shih Tzu Club. The Brownriggs were instrumental in founding the Club and with General Sir Douglas Brownrigg as Hon Treasurer and Lady Brownrigg as Hon Secretary, the Club went from strength to strength.

During the early years the Shih Tzu Club sponsored classes at many of the Championship Shows, helping the breed to attract a good deal of attention. The war years were difficult ones but once it had ended Mrs Garforth-Bless (now Mrs Widdrington) became Hon Treasurer and helped Lady Brownrigg to get the Club back on its feet. Lady Brownrigg was to remain Secretary of the Club until 1954, when she took over as President. The current Hon Secretary and Hon Treasurer is Mrs Josephine Johnson, President is Mrs Audrey Dadds and Chairman, Mr Ken Rawlings. There is now a membership of over three hundred.

THE MANCHU SHIH TZU SOCIETY

Although the Manchu Shih Tzu Society was founded in 1956, it was not until 1962 that the Kennel Club granted recognition. Thus it was that in 1987 the Society held its Silver Jubilee with the late Thelma Morgan and the late Stan Gurney as judges on the prestigious occasion of the year's Championship Show.

A Special General Meeting was held in 1962 at the Queen's Hotel in Birmingham and the first Officers of the Society were Mrs L G Widdrington as President, Mr A O Grindey as Chairman with Mrs S M Bode as Hon Secretary and Mr C B Newson Treasurer. From then on Annual General Meetings were held in London, firstly in hotels but subsequently at the Kennel Club. However in 1979 it was decided that the Meetings should be held alternately in London and in Birmingham and in 1980 the members voted to hold all future AGM's in the Midlands, something which has continued up to the present day.

When Kennel Club recognition had been granted the Manchu began regularly to organise shows for the breed, the first Championship event being in 1969 with Mrs Olive Newson, breed specialist, as the judge at this important show. Since then there has been a Championship Show each year as well as Open Shows, of which there are presently two per year.

Much of the income from members' subscriptions goes into the publication of newsletters, the object being to educate and inform members about the Shih Tzu and its care. Newsletters also provide an important point of contact between members wherever they live. Material of this kind has been published since the Society's earliest beginnings in 1957 and now there are two publications each year. In 1981 the Manchu collaborated with the Shih Tzu Club in compiling and publishing an illustrated list of "British Shih Tzu Champions, 1949-1980", something which has become an invaluable source of reference to students of the breed. Mrs Val Goodwin is the present Hon Secretary of the Manchu Shih Tzu Society.

THE SHIH TZU CLUB OF SCOTLAND

It was late in 1979 and early in 1980 that a group of breed enthusiasts got together in Scotland to form the Shih Tzu Club of Scotland, its aim being to try to promote and protect the breed's interest in Scotland. With the support of the Scottish Kennel Club, the Manchu Shih Tzu Society and the Shih Tzu Club, who made a gift of £100, the new club quickly got off the ground. From the beginning, one of the Club's policies has been to protect the breed from abuse and to deter over-breeding, officials and committee members keeping a vigilant eye on puppy advertisements and being careful about the use of stud dogs. The Club also has a policy of promoting new names for its Championship Shows and for its first such event invited Mrs Erna Jungafeldt from Sweden. The Club is grateful that Mrs Widdrington, its Patron, has supported the Club in many ways from the outset and is a frequent visitor at shows. Mrs Margaret Turnbull is President and Mr Jim Peat has been Chairman since the Club's inception. The first Hon Secretary was Mr Philip Martin and that office is now held by Mrs Vicki Grugan.

NORTHERN COUNTIES SHIH TZU CLUB

The Northern Counties Shih Tzu Club was formed and approved by the Kennel Club in 1981 to serve the needs of the breed in the North. Founder Hon Secretary of the Club is Mr R. Metcalfe who still continues this office, Chairman is Mr H S Baxter, President Mrs M Grace and Treasurer Mr B Medforth. The Club holds two Open Shows and one Championship show each year and each of the shows is at a different venue, covering the region. There are other events such as rallies and teach-ins for potential judges. The Club's Rescue officer is Mrs E Macdonald whose husband is, very conveniently, a vet.

The Northern Counties Club has also produced a Limited Edition Book of British Champions, this in 1991. It is a high quality, loose-leaf publication and the Club's aim is to update it at regular intervals. Cruft's 1992 was a busy time for the Club for it produced the first issue of a most informative European Shih Tzu Year Book and also organised a successful Seminar and 'Supermatch' the same weekend.

THE SHIH TZU CLUB OF SOUTH WALES AND WESTERN COUNTIES

The Shih Tzu Club of South Wales and Western Counties held its inaugural meeting in 1983 and Kennel Club recognition was granted in January of the following year. In September of that same year the Club held its first Open Show and indeed it was a busy year for the new Club for it also held a talk on Tibetan Breeds. The Club's first Championship event came in 1988.

The Club's Patron is Mr David Samuel, its President Mr Elywn Harding and the Hon Secretary is Mrs Diana B Harding. The Club now has a membership figure of 130 and continues to hold shows and other events for those interested in the breed.